A Korean Mother's Cooking Notes

A Korean Mother's Cooking Notes

Chang Sun-young
Translated by Kim Miza

Ewha Womans University Press

A Korean Mother's Cooking Notes
by Chang Sun-young
translated by Kim Miza

Copyright © 1997 by Ewha Womans University Press

First published 10 May, 1997
Eighth printing 15 December, 2008
Published by Ewha Womans University Press
11-1 Daehyun-dong, Seodaemun-gu, Seoul, Korea 120-750
Tel. (82-2)3277-3164, 362-6076
Fax. (82-2)312-4312
E-mail : press@ewha.ac.kr
Online bookstore : www.ewhapress.com

Price : 14,000won
ISBN 978-89-7300-299-3 23590

CONTENTS

Rice Pap, 밥

Soup   Kuk, 국

Clear Soup (Soup without soybean paste)

Soybean Paste Soup *(Toenjang kuk)*

Stew Tchigae, 찌개

Food Boiled or Fried in Sauce
Chorim, 조림 and Pokkŭm, 볶음

Braised and Steamed Food   Tchim, 찜

Broiled Food   Kui, 구이

Pan-Fried Foods Chŏnya, 저냐

Rice Porridge Chuk, 죽

Pickled Food Chang-atchi, 장아찌

Vegetable Dishes Namul, 나물

Kimch'i 김치

Popular Dishes

Desserts

Dinner Guests

Food for Babies

Food for Special Days

You must be breathlessly busy, raising babies, doing household chores and attending the university. And then there is the business of cooking meal after meal, day after day. It would be a little easier if you had a pre-set menu, but even then, to make things taste the way you want them is another matter. Luckily, the men in our family are not gourmets and, bless them, not very difficult to please.

I didn't have to cook for a long time after I got married because I worked and my sister in Champaign, who used to live next door, did all the cooking. She was such a good cook there was no room for me in our small kitchen. I was truly helpless when I left my job and tried to cook myself. Whenever I asked my sister how to do something, she would simply say, "Oh, you just do it. There's nothing to teach," but was there a lot to learn! It was most frustrating, but she taught me how to season and spice things properly so I managed more or less to turn out dishes that tasted almost, if not exactly, as they should. Looking back to those times, I have written down as much as I can remember about the little difficulties I had in the hope the information will help you. I have tried to make the information easy to understand.

Because my favorite recipes may not be your favorites, I tried to select only those that are easy to cook. You may already have a great many cookbooks with beautifully colored pictures, but it won't hurt to add this less-flashy cookbook to your collection.

Eating together at home is the best way to make a family close. You can also teach your children table manners when you have meals together. Children who grow up without having a warm rapport with their parents will most probably turn into parents no better than theirs. I am sure the short cut to a warm, close family is having meals together. The joy of working in the kitchen and setting the table for their family is a lesson children can learn only from their parents. As the saying goes, good families make good communities, good communities make good nations and good nations make a good world.

I think the most important ingredient in making food is a caring heart. You will always end up with unsavory food if you cook with indifference or regard cooking as a boring chore. Always cook with the same caring spirit artists give their work.

The next most important thing is proper seasoning. Regardless of how nice a dish might look, it will be a flop if it is not seasoned properly. Always measure soy sauce, salt and other basic condiments. Don't add them carelessly, tasting and adding, again and again. The end result will be tasteless. Of course, it will be a different story when you have become an expert cook. You will then know how much to add without measuring.

It's not just clothes that are sensitive to fashion. One tends to cook things that are in fashion and forget old recipes, but seasoning holds for both fashionable and outdated dishes.

I have double-checked my recipes by measuring the seasonings again each time. I expect the dishes will taste the same as those you have had at my house if you follow my measurements faithfully. However, the joy of cooking is in doing it one's own way. For your own sense of fulfillment, I suggest you sprinkle my recipes with your creativity.

You have heard that the best medicine is food. That means that eating properly and with relish can do far greater things for your health than all kinds of so-called invigorating medicines. Some people tend to follow every health food fad, but the most healthful diet is the one that makes you want to eat everything.

Eating out can be a fun change but you can't do it every day. Besides, no restaurant meal is a match for a home cooked one prepared with a caring heart. What counts about a meal is not what it is but how it is made and eaten. It should be eaten with all of the family around the table sharing not only food but their love for each other. I am sure we would have far fewer juvenile problems if parents ate with their children. I read in a newspaper about a poll of high school students which revealed that they liked their mothers' cooking best. Food a mother cooks for her children is far more valuable than any money she gives them to eat out.

After each meal, it would be nice if each member of the family would take his or her own dishes to the sink, clean the table and, better still, wash and dry dishes together. Household chores should be shared between husband and wife. Even in Korea, the distinction between men's work and women's work is diminishing. Still, some might protest that it is unfair to make a man work at home when he has worked all day at his job, but you and I both know that we are not playing at home. Besides, doing household chores would be a healthy way for him to relax after a stressful day at the office and give him a chance to chat about the day with his family.

Starting married life in America must be hard for a bride who grew up in Korea, especially since you can't call your mother for help whenever you have trouble as most brides do in Seoul. However, you will become skilled very fast.

Bear in mind that the ingredients and their preparation, the measurements, the cooking procedures and the hints I have written here are just for reference. If you find better, easier ways, write them down in the margin. I know you are good cooks, but hopefully my recipes will help you when you can't decide what to cook for your next meal. This is a collection of everyday cooking, not special dishes for parties, although I have included some recipes for special occasions just in case.

I hope the comments and cooking hints I have jotted down here and there will help you as you start your own homes in America, away from the familiar environment of Korea where you grew up. However, don't feel obligated to do things a certain way because that is how your mother-in-law does them. As I have not been blessed with daughters, you two are more like daughters to me than daughters-in-law. If you are already familiar with the things I have written, just consider this as an old mother's way of welcoming you, which I do with open arms and joy.

The measurements used in all the recipes here are for ingredients – soy sauce, sugar and other seasonings – available in Seoul. They may need to be adjusted for seasonings available in America.

Because garlic, green onions and ginger go into almost every Korean food, I suggest you clean them immediately after you have done the grocery shopping and sort them in vegetable boxes. Chop garlic and green onions in your spare time and keep them in small jars for ready use. You will find this saves time and makes cooking more enjoyable.

Everyday cooking does not consume much time because you don't have to cook many things, and furthermore nothing has to be ready on the dot. However, cooking for dinner guests can be quite nerve racking because you have to prepare many special dishes by a deadline. To keep from having to wash the cutting board and open and close the refrigerator every few minutes, try to streamline your cooking. Write down the menu and keep it somewhere you can see easily. Prepare ingredients by kind. For example, do all the vegetables first, then the seafood and then the meat. That way you will need to clean the cutting board only when you are finished with each kind of ingredient and not after each ingredient.

The recipes in this book are for four servings, unless otherwise specified. You might find some quite inadequate for four people but you must remember most Korean foods are side dishes. We have quite a different concept of main dishes from Westerners – the real main dishes being always rice and soup. Everything else is a side dish to help diners consume them with relish. Because there are usually a number of side dishes for one meal, each does not have to come in as large a quantity as a Western main dish.

Grocery Shopping

I don't mean grocery shopping for parties or special occasions because these involve the purchase of things specific for each occasion. What I mean is shopping for things that won't spoil in a short period of time and are needed for everyday cooking, such as flour, sesame oil, salad oil, soy sauce, salt and sugar. You wouldn't want to have to rush out to the nearest shop for one of these while making food.

It's convenient to have a specific day for grocery shopping. Get the week's vegetables, wash what needs to be washed and store them by kind. I wouldn't buy more than needed, even though the price is irresistible, for a bargain is often no gain at all if it goes stale or rots because you have more than you can actually use.

I like to do my shopping at the Karak Wholesale Market in Seoul but there is one problem with shopping there — they won't sell in small quantities. Vegetable vendors especially tend to give a lot even when I ask them for less than the money's worth. Vegetables take up so much space in the refrigerator and think about the electric bill! Nevertheless, I often end up buying more than needed because I live so far away from shops. Cucumbers go bad in 3 or 4 days. There are only so many days each kind of vegetable can keep fresh in the refrigerator. You can keep carrots and celery longer if you keep them, unwashed, wrapped in newspaper. It's better to cook or make pickles of the things you have bought more than enough of. But then, the best way is to buy just the amount you really need.

The following measurements are for reference:

1 Korean *kŭn* equals 600 grams
1 pound (16 ounces) is 453 grams
1 ounce is 28 grams
1 cup equals 16 tablespoons or 8 ounces
1 tablespoon is 3 teaspoons
1 cup of minced meat is 200 grams

Green Onion *(P'a,* 파)

This is the most often used ingredient so it's a good idea to store chopped ones in a jar in the refrigerator. Don't worry if you have bought more than enough; wrap the extra, uncleaned, with newspaper and store in a plastic container. Green onions will stay fresh for a long time. If you are going to store green onions after washing, don't cut the root completely off for the inner layers might slip out if they are not held in place by the root.

When chopping green onions, slice through the lower white part lengthwise several times before slicing it across. This makes chopping faster and easier. The roots can be used also, but they should be washed thoroughly. Add them when boiling pork to eliminate the odor of the pork. The roots also make the juice of radish water *kimch'i (tongch'imi kimch'i)* fresher.

Garlic *(Manŭl,* 마늘)

Keep peeled garlic in a plastic container, or chop perhaps a week's supply in advance and keep it in a small jar for handy use. Don't crush it with the bottom of the knife handle. It is easier to break it with the back of the knife before chopping. Some people crush it with a hand-squeezer but I find washing the squeezer a bigger chore. The best, if not the easiest way, is to slice and chop. That way the garlic odor will not linger.

The Chinese make the job look very easy. They just whack unpeeled cloves with the broadside of a huge knife and chop them several times, and that's it. Of course, minced garlic can be purchased but who knows how clean it is?

You can use any amount of garlic in boiled dishes, but be careful when preparing a fresh dish because you might find yourself in an embarrassing situation because of the odor. After all, the amount of garlic does not proportionately increase the taste of the food. Buddhist monks in temples never use garlic but their food is very delicious!

Ginger *(Saenggang,* 생강*)*

Keep peeled ginger in a plastic container in the refrigerator. American ginger is so big it can be peeled like an apple.

I cut ginger into thin slices and then mash them. I wrap the slices in plastic wrap before mashing so I won't have the chore of cleaning the cutting board.

Roasted Whole Sesame *(T'ongkkae,* 통깨*)* and Sesame Salt *(Kkaesogŭm,* 깨소금*)*

Soak sesame seeds in water, scrub and sieve them to remove grit. Don't wash them like you would rice because they will float away. Let the ones that float up after soaking and scrubbing float away, however, because they are hollow shells. Sieve only the ones that settle to the bottom.

Brown the drained seeds in a heavy skillet, first over a high flame, stirring from time to time. When they are dry and begin to pop, lower the flame. The sesame is roasted well when the popping stops. Another way to tell is to try to crush some seeds between your fingers; they should crush easily. Don't leave them in the pan because they will keep cooking even after you turn off the fire. Keep stirring until the pan cools or remove the seeds from the pan.

We need both whole and ground sesame. Keep half of the roasted sesame seeds in a jar and grind the rest until they are half crushed. No salt is added but we call it sesame salt, perhaps to differentiate it from the whole.

Salt *(Sogŭm,* 소금)

There is very fine salt, refined salt and crude salt, but I refer only to the first two here. These days, I roast crude salt and crush it into powder myself. I think it tastes better. You might be able to find roasted salt in shops. The measurement is about the same as fine salt. Remember American table salt (such as Morton salt) is twice as salty as Korean fine salt. Unless specified otherwise, I mean the latter or the roasted salt when I say "salt."

Pine Nut Powder *(Chat karu,* 잣가루)

Finely chopped pine nut is useful for garnishing meat dishes, *kujŏlp'an* (nine-section dish), and other sophisticated dishes. Sprinkled on before serving, it makes simple *pulgogi* (broiled beef) look quite classy. Its major drawback is the price, but pine nuts are said to convert animal fat to vegetable fat, so the price can be forgiven.

Remove the tops from the skinned nuts. Spread a paper towel over the cutting board and chop the nuts, with your free hand pressing down on the tip of the knife. Shuffle them around on the paper towel every now and then as you chop them so that the grease from the nuts soaks into the towel. When the nuts are chopped fine enough, wrap them in a fresh paper towel, place in a plastic bag and keep in the freezer.

(I have recently found that a rotary grater Americans use to grate cheese does a wonderful job in making pine nut powder!)

Soy Sauce

There are two kinds of soy sauce *(kanjang):* the clear "soup soy sauce" *(kuk kanjang),* so called because it is used mostly in making soup; and the regular "pure soy sauce" *(chin kanjang),* used for braising and most other dishes. The regular type is darker and less salty than the clear type. I mean the regular type when I say "soy sauce."

Kikkoman, the Japanese soy sauce prevalent in American shops, is saltier than regular Korean soy sauce *(chin kanjang)* so it is a good idea to lighten it with sugar and honey. Mix 2 cups Kikkoman with $\frac{2}{3}$ cup sugar and $\frac{1}{2}$ cup honey. It is a very handy sauce.

Vinegar Soy Sauce *(Ch'o kanjang)*

1 tablespoon soy sauce
2 teaspoons vinegar
$\frac{1}{2}$ teaspoon sugar

Depending on the dish, add red pepper powder, sesame salt or ground pine nuts.

Vinegar Red Pepper Paste *(Ch'o koch'ujang)*

2 tablespoons red pepper paste
1 tablespoon honey
1 tablespoon vinegar

Sugar or starch syrup *(mullyŏt)* can be used instead of honey.

Grilled Beef *(Pulgogi)* Sauce
— For 1 pound sliced meat

3 tablespoons soy sauce
2 tablespoons sugar
1 tablespoon honey
2 tablespoons wine
1 tablespoon sesame oil
3 tablespoons chopped green onions
2 teaspoons chopped garlic
1 teaspoon pepper
1 tablespoon sesame salt

Sauces for Braising (Chorimjang)

Boil the following ingredients to make the sauce and keep them on hand to make spicy braised dishes (chorim).

For Braised Pork Ribs
(Toeji kalbi kangjŏng)
— 1 pound pork ribs

3 tablespoons soy sauce
2 tablespoons sugar
2 tablespoons rice wine or red wine
1 tablespoon honey
1 tablespoon sesame oil
2 or 3 cloves garlic, sliced
sliced ginger

Add dried red peppers (not ground) for spicy flavor. If not available, red pepper paste (koch'ujang) will do (at the proportion of 1 tablespoon koch'ujang to 2 tablespoons soy sauce).

For Braised Chicken (Tak kangjŏng)
— 1 pound chicken

2 tablespoons soy sauce
1 tablespoon koch'ujang *(Add another tablespoon of soy sauce if dried pepper is used in place of* koch'ujang*)*
2 tablespoons sugar
1 tablespoon honey
2 tablespoons wine
1 tablespoon sesame oil
2 or 3 cloves of garlic
sliced ginger

For Braised Fish (Saengsŏn chorim)
— 1 pound fish with bones

2 tablespoons soy sauce
1 tablespoon koch'ujang
1 tablespoon sugar
1 tablespoon wine
1 tablespoon cooking wine or $\frac{1}{2}$ tablespoon vinegar
thinly sliced garlic and ginger

Sauce for Fresh Vegetables, especially Korean Cabbage (Paech'u)

2 tablespoons soy sauce
2 tablespoons vinegar
2 tablespoons sugar
2 tablespoons anchovy sauce (myŏlch'i chŏt)
1 tablespoon red pepper powder
1 tablespoon sesame salt
2 tablespoons chopped green onions
$\frac{1}{4}$ teaspoon chopped garlic (Sliced fresh garlic leaves can be substituted)

Sprinkle the mixture over thoroughly washed, fresh vegetables, torn into bite-size pieces.

Sauce for Chestnut Salad (Pam much'im)

1 tablespoon salt (1 teaspoon table salt)
5 tablespoons sugar
3 tablespoons vinegar
2 tablespoons red pepper powder

Mustard Sauce

1 tablespoon Chinese mustard (prepared and sold in a tube)
3 tablespoons vinegar
3 tablespoons sugar
1 teaspoon salt

Flavored Soybean Paste (Mattoenjang)

$\frac{1}{2}$ cup soybean paste (toenjang)
1 tablespoon ground anchovy (myŏlch'i)
1 tablespoon sesame oil
1 teaspoon minced garlic
1 tablespoon flour
$\frac{1}{2}$ cup water

Pour sesame oil and garlic in a heated pan, add ground anchovy, stir-fry. Pass *toenjang* through a sieve pressing it with a spoon and add to the above ingredients. After some more stir-frying, mix flour with water and add to *toenjang*. Boil the mixture until it becomes thick. Put in a storage jar when cooled.

I fry ground *myŏlch'i* with sesame oil and garlic to remove the fishy smell of the *myŏlch'i*. This flavored soybean paste is very handy when making stew (tchigae) or soup (kuk).

You can make a delightfully quick bean paste stew *(toenjang tchigae)* with *mattoenjang*:

$\frac{1}{4}$ *cup ground beef*
2 or 3 tablespoons mattoenjang
$\frac{1}{2}$ *cup bean curd* (tubu)
2 or 3 fresh green peppers
2 cups water

Stir-fry beef, add fresh green peppers, cut to $\frac{1}{2}$ inch lengths, water and *mattoenjang*. When it comes to a boil, add bean curd *(tubu),* cut into $\frac{1}{2}$ inch cubes. Bring to a second boil, and you have a delicious *toenjang tchigae.*

With this flavored soybean paste, you can also make *ssamjang* to go with lettuce or other fresh vegetables:

$\frac{1}{2}$ *cup* mattoenjang
$\frac{1}{4}$ *cup red pepper paste* (koch'ujang)
$\frac{1}{2}$ *cup ground beef*
1 tablespoon sesame oil
1 teaspoon chopped garlic
$\frac{1}{4}$ *teaspoon pepper*

Stir-fry ground beef with sesame oil, chopped garlic, and pepper, then add *mattoenjang* and red pepper paste *(koch'ujang).* Stir-fry 1 or 2 more minutes. Some people make *ssamjang*

with anchovy sauce *(myŏlch'i chŏt)* and red pepper powder, but I find it too salty.

Another way to make *Ssamjang*
A. $\frac{1}{4}$ *cup bean paste*
    2 tablespoons red pepper paste (koch'ujang)
    1 tablespoon sesame oil
    1 tablespoon ground anchovy
    $\frac{1}{2}$ *tablespoon chopped garlic*
    1 tablespoon flour
    $\frac{1}{4}$ *cup water*

B. $\frac{1}{4}$ *cup ground beef*
    $\frac{1}{2}$ *teaspoon chopped garlic*
    $\frac{1}{2}$ *teaspoon sugar*
    1 tablespoon sesame oil
    $\frac{1}{4}$ *cup grated onion*
    1 tablespoon chopped green peppers (optional)
    $\frac{1}{2}$ *cup bean curd (optional)*
    $\frac{1}{2}$ *cup Chinese chives* (puch'u), *cut to 1 inch lengths*

A. Press bean paste through a sieve. Pour sesame oil in a pan and stir-fry ground anchovy and chopped garlic. Add sieved bean paste and red pepper paste. Add the mixture of flour and water and bring to a boil.

B. In another pan, stir-fry ground beef, garlic, sugar and sesame oil. Add grated onion. When the onion is cooked, add the above (A) mixture. You might want to add chopped green peppers and/or bean curd, crushed or strained, when the mixture is boiling hard.

Stir from time to time to prevent burning. When almost all liquid has boiled down, add Chinese chives, cut in short lengths. Chives enhance the flavor but when you don't have them on hand, use chopped green onions.
Add a drop of sesame oil and sprinkle sesame salt just before serving.

Note
When I serve lettuce for wrapping rice *(sangch'u ssam)* with *ssamjang* and sometimes *ch'o koch'ujang* (red bean paste flavored with vinegar, chopped garlic and green onion, and sugar), I also prepare *pulgogi* (grilled beef) or broiled beef to go with it. Canned tuna, drained well and sautéed with chopped green onion, red pepper powder and a little bit of soup soy sauce *(kuk kanjang),* is also very good when wrapped with *ssamjang* in lettuce.

Sautéed Red Pepper Paste (*Pokkŭm koch'ujang*)

1 cup ground beef
2 cups red pepper paste
1 tablespoon sesame oil
1 teaspoon chopped garlic
$\frac{1}{4}$ cup honey
$\frac{1}{4}$ cup sugar
1 tablespoon whole, roasted sesame
  or 1 tablespoon pine nuts

Mix ground meat with sesame oil and chopped garlic. Stir-fry. When the meat is cooked, add red pepper paste and bring to a boil, stirring constantly. Add honey and sugar when the mixture is boiling hard and bring to a second boil. Turn off the heat and add sesame or pine nuts.

Note
If red pepper paste is already sweet, add less sugar. Be prepared when you sauté a large quantity of red pepper paste. It splatters everywhere. It's best to cover the kitchen floor with newspaper and also tape some on the walls and counter top.

If you want to add pine nuts instead of sesame, use whole ones because they make the sautéed red pepper paste crunchy. Besides, pine nut powder tends to become stale quickly.

RECIPES

Rice *Pap*, 밥

 Pronounced like the "pap" in "papa", *pap* (cooked rice) is the staple of Koreans. Nowadays some Koreans have a Western style breakfast of toast and coffee, but before the introduction of bread and butter, rice, cooked with or without other grains, was a must for all three daily meals and it still is for many Koreans. Elderly people click their tongues at young people who prefer pastry and noodles to rice and say, "You won't be strong and energetic without rice inside you."

You would think all you need to do to cook rice is boil it in water, but cooking rice well is not such a simple job, especially when you have guests and have to cook more than you ordinarily do for your family. Cooking rice has become much simpler with the advent of the electric rice cooker, but still you can easily end up with more or less rice than you need.

I have written a quick recipe for cooking rice and some recipes for rice dishes which are enough by themselves and thus need no side dishes.

Cooked Rice　*Hŭin pap,* 흰밥

2 cups rice
2 cups water

1. Wash and soak rice for 1 hour.

2. Place rice in a pan and cover with the same amount of water as rice. If the rice is not soaked, add a quarter more water for each cup.

3. When the rice begins to boil, stir once with a spatula and replace the cover.

4. Lower the heat, stir again when it comes to a boil and simmer on low heat.

Rice with Five Grains　*Ogok pap,* 오곡밥

1 cup regular rice (**ssal**)
1 cup glutinous rice (**ch'ap ssal**)
$\frac{1}{4}$ *cup black beans* (**k'ong**)
$\frac{1}{4}$ *cup sweet beans* (**p'at**)
$\frac{1}{4}$ *cup glutinous sorghum* (**ch'a susu**)
$\frac{1}{4}$ *cup glutinous millet* (**ch'a cho**)
1 teaspoon table salt

1. Wash glutinous sorghum and soak in water for a day, changing the water occasionally to remove bitter taste.

2. Wash and soak regular and glutinous rice in water for 4 hours and drain.

3. Soak black beans in water for 4 hours or longer and drain.

4. Wash sweet beans, bring to a quick boil and drain. Cook in water until the beans become the size of fresh beans. Save the water in which the beans were boiled and add 1 teaspoon of salt to each cup of water.

5. Mix all the ingredients except the millet. Place the mixture in a pot and cover it with red bean water and, if needed, plain water. Whereas you normally need 1 cup of water for each cup of rice, you will need less water because of the glutinous rice. Take out 3 tablespoons from each cup of water.

6. When the rice mixture comes to a boil, add the millet and simmer. The millet will float to the top and stick to the inside of the cover if you add it from the beginning.

Note

Salt is a must for *ogok pap.*

Be sure not to boil the sweet beans too long because they will become shapeless when cooked with rice.

You can steam the rice and grain mixture instead of cooking it in a pan. Spread a hemp cloth on the steamer and place the mixture on it when the water is boiling hard. Regular rice should not be used because it will not cook well. When the grain mixture is almost cooked, sprinkle salt water over it. The glutinous rice will turn a pretty color when you cook it in a pan. But for steaming, you should soak it in the sweet bean water to give it a nice color.

Vegetables Mixed with Rice
Pibim pap, 비빔밥

You don't need to prepare all of the following ingredients. Four or five vegetables and fried beef will be sufficient.

6 cups rice, soaked
½ pound lean beef (1 cup when sliced)
3 oak mushrooms (**p'yogo**)
½ cup carrot, sliced
1 cup onion, sliced
1 cup bellflower roots (**toraji**)
2 cups cucumber, sliced
2 cups bean sprouts
2 cups young shoots of bracken (**kosari**)
salt, soy sauce, green onion, garlic, ginger, sesame salt, sesame oil, cooking oil, pepper, pear, soup stock

1. Rice for *pibim pap* should be a little drier than usual. Usually 1 cup water is needed to cook 1 cup of soaked rice but, for this recipe, use 2 tablespoons less water.

2. Cut beef across the grain into fine, 2-inch-long strips. Season the meat with 1 tablespoon each soy sauce, pear juice, chopped green onion and sesame salt; 2 teaspoons each sugar and sesame oil; 1 teaspoon chopped garlic; $\frac{1}{4}$ teaspoon ginger juice; and $\frac{1}{4}$ teaspoon pepper. Stir-fry.

3. Soak mushrooms. Cut into thin slices, season with 1 tablespoon *pulgogi* sauce, and stir-fry.

4. Peel carrot and slice into 2-inch-long strips. Stir-fry in a hot oiled pan, adding $\frac{1}{4}$ teaspoon table salt. Carrots become discolored when fried in oil only. Add water by spoonfuls while stir-frying.

5. Cut onions to the size of carrot strips. Stir-fry the same as carrot, adding $\frac{1}{2}$ teaspoon table salt.

6. Scald bellflower roots in salt water. Stir-fry, adding $\frac{1}{2}$ teaspoon crushed garlic, $\frac{1}{2}$ teaspoon table salt and a dash of pepper. Add 3 to 4 tablespoons beef stock or water. When tender, remove from heat, and mix with chopped green onion, sesame salt and a drop of sesame oil.

7. Cut cucumber into chunks 2 inches long, peel the skin off carefully and slice the skin into thin strips. (Do not use the soft flesh inside.) Sprinkle with $\frac{1}{2}$ tablespoon table salt and let stand. When limp, squeeze hard and stir-fry.

8. In a hot pan, fry $\frac{1}{2}$ teaspoon chopped garlic in 1 teaspoon cooking oil, add bean sprouts and $\frac{1}{2}$ teaspoon table salt, and stir. Cover and simmer until bean sprouts are well cooked. Turn off the heat and season with 1 tablespoon each sesame oil, sesame salt and chopped green onion, and $\frac{1}{2}$ teaspoon red pepper powder.

Vegetables Mixed with Rice
Pibim pap

37

9. Cut bracken into 2-inch-long pieces. Season with 2 teaspoons soup soy sauce *(kuk kanjang)*, 2 teaspoons dark soy sauce *(chin kanjang)*, 2 teaspoons chopped garlic, 2 teaspoons cooking oil, and $\frac{1}{2}$ teaspoon pepper. Stir-fry awhile, then add beef stock or water to cover and simmer. Mix with 1 tablespoon each green onion strips, sesame salt and sesame oil.

10. To serve, place a scoop of rice in a bowl and sprinkle with 2 teaspoons sesame oil. Arrange above vegetables side by side on the rice, with 1 teaspoon seasoned red pepper paste.
Makes 8 servings.

Note

Some people like to have a fried egg, sunny side up, on the vegetables and mix it together with everything else. Mixing in strips of pear will make *pibim pap* very delicious. You might also like adding strips of radish, salted, squeezed and stir-fried. Fried kelp *(tashima)* is also very nice but it is rather boring to cut it into strips. Asian grocery stores sell bags of thread-thin strips of *tashima*. Fry them at home and sprinkle over the rice.

Kimch'i and Bean Sprouts to Mix with Rice
Kimch'i k'ongnamul pap, 김치콩나물밥

2 cups rice
3 cups bean sprouts
$\frac{1}{2}$ pound (1 cup) sliced beef or pork
1 cup (sliced and squeezed) **kimch'i**
1 tablespoon sesame oil

A. 1 tablespoon soy sauce
   1 teaspoon sugar
   1 teaspoon chopped garlic
   1 teaspoon sesame oil
   $\frac{1}{2}$ teaspoon black pepper
   1 teaspoon ginger juice (for pork)

B. 2 tablespoons soy sauce
   2 tablespoons chopped green onion
   1 tablespoon sesame oil
   1 tablespoon sesame salt
   1 teaspoon chopped garlic
   1 teaspoon red pepper powder

1. Wash rice and bean sprouts.

2. Cut beef or pork into strips. Season with (A) ingredients. Add 1 teaspoon ginger juice for pork.

3. Remove stuffing from *kimch'i*. Cut *kimch'i* into small pieces and squeeze. Mix with seasoned meat. In a pot or electric rice cooker, place a layer of *kimch'i* and meat mixture, a layer of soaked rice, and repeat. Pour $1\frac{3}{4}$ cups water or, if you want

softer rice, 2 cups water for 2 cups rice. When the rice begins to boil, lower the heat. Add bean sprouts when the water simmers down and keep on very low heat until the bean sprouts are done. Add sesame oil and mix well before serving.

4. Mix (B) ingredients for the *yangnyŏmjang* to serve with the *k'ongnamul pap*.

Note

If the *kimch'i* is too sour, wash it in water before cutting into pieces. Season with red pepper paste, cooking oil and sugar before mixing with meat.

Be sure not to use too much water when cooking the rice because water will come out of the bean sprouts. If you cook bean sprouts with the rice from the beginning, they will become stringy.

10 full-sized sheets of laver (**kim**)
2 cups soaked rice
$\frac{1}{3}$ pound beef
2 eggs
1 cucumber or $\frac{1}{2}$ bundle spinach
1 pickled radish (**tanmuji** *or* **takuan**)
1 carrot
5 oak mushrooms (**p'yogo**)
pulgogi sauce (page 27)
vinegar, sugar, salt, cooking wine, anchovy stock (page 42)

1. Heat a mixture of $\frac{1}{4}$ cup vinegar, 3 tablespoons sugar and 1 teaspoon table salt until it bubbles.

2. Cook rice with $1\frac{3}{4}$ cup water. When the rice is cooked, add (1) mixture and mix.

3. Cut the cucumbers and carrots the same length as the laver sheets and cut them into strips $\frac{1}{4}$ inch thick and wide. Soak the strips in a mixture of $\frac{1}{2}$ cup vinegar, $\frac{1}{2}$ cup sugar and 1 teaspoon table salt. Cut the pickled radish the same way.

4. Beat eggs well with a little salt. Fry the egg in thick sheets on medium to low heat. Cut to the size of the pickled radish strips.

5. Cut beef into sheets, marinate in *pulgogi* sauce, and fry. Cut fried meat to the size of radish strips.

6. Trim and blanch the spinach. Squeeze out the water and mix with the salt.

7. Soak mushrooms in lukewarm water for about 20 minutes until they soften. Remove stems and cut into $\frac{1}{4}$-inch-thick pieces. Add 2 tablespoons soy sauce, 2 tablespoons sugar and 2 tablespoons cooking wine to the water in which the mushrooms were soaked (the water will be enough if it barely covers the mushroom slices) and simmer.

8. Roast laver sheets very lightly. Place a sheet on the bamboo mat, spread a thin layer of vinegared rice on it, leaving about one-third of the sheet farthest from you uncovered. Lay the strips of beef and vegetables at the center of the rice. Roll it up as you would a jelly roll by rolling the bamboo mat. The uncovered part of the laver will seal the roll.

9. Cut the rolls into $\frac{1}{2}$-inch-thick slices to serve or pack into lunch boxes.

Note

This is very good for picnics. You don't have to prepare all of the above vegetables. Four or five that will make the rolls colorful when cut are enough. For example, you don't need to use both spinach and cucumber — either of the two will do. *Kimch'i* makes very good stuffing when cut into lengths, squeezed and mixed with sesame oil and sesame salt.

For children, cut the laver sheets into half to make thin rolls.

You can make raw fish sushi with the vinegared rice. Get pieces of fish prepared for raw fish dishes and also Japanese mustard *(wasabi)*. Or make *inari sushi* by stuffing the rice in fried bean curd *(aburage)*. The *inari sushi* shells that come out of a can are too sweet. I suggest you squeeze them hard and simmer in soy sauce and sugar before stuffing them.

Soup Kuk, 국

Soup is served before the main course in the West and also in China but we serve it together with the other dishes. Actually, soup and a bowl of rice is often all Koreans need. A delicious soup and some well-seasoned *kimch'i* or *kkaktugi* can make a meal quite sumptuous.

Soup is very important. Many Koreans think they have not had a proper meal if it lacks a bowl of soup or at least a soupy stew *(tchigae)*. I wonder if you have experienced the soothing feeling a bowl of soup gives you when you are so tired you don't care to eat anything else? I think Korean soup contains some curious potion that settles one's nerves.

Soup can be categorized as clear soup, soybean paste soup *(toenjang kuk)* and salted soup. Clear soup seems to go better with *pibim pap* (rice mixed with vegetables) and *kimch'i pap* (rice mixed with *kimch'i*), but I think *toenjang kuk* is better for braised, roasted or broiled dishes

The most important thing for good soup is a good soup stock. Save and store in the freezer the fat you trim from beef. It makes good soup stock, especially when a package of bones is added. I have found that using different kinds of beef together makes a better stock than using one kind of beef. The stock is very handy whether you make clear soup or soybean paste soup.

To make beef stock

2 pounds beef
30 to 35 cups water

Put the meat in cold water and boil until it becomes very tender. Strain. Don't skim off the fat. When cool, store it in the refrigerator. The fat will harden into an airtight lid and keep the stock from spoiling for a long time. When you want to use the stock, just remove the hardened fat and heat.

To make anchovy stock

1 cup dried, large anchovies
2 dry oak mushrooms (p'yogo)
kelp (tashima), *about the size of your palm*
8 cups water

Soak the ingredients in cold water for 2 to 3 hours. Bring to a boil, uncovered, over a high heat. After it boils for 2 or 3 minutes, turn off the heat and let cool. When the stock is cooled, pass through a sieve. Be sure to leave the pot uncovered when you boil anchovies for the fishy odor will linger if you cover it.

Seaweed Soup   *Miyŏk kuk,* 미역국

2 cups soaked and drained seaweed (**miyŏk**)
3 cups soup stock
2 teaspoons chopped garlic
1 tablespoon sesame oil
1 teaspoon soup soy sauce (**kuk kanjang**)
1 teaspoon salt

Pour sesame oil in a heated pan and stir-fry *miyŏk* with garlic, sesame oil, soup soy sauce and salt. When *miyŏk* sizzles, add 1 cup soup stock. Repeat the process until you have added 3 cups soup stock. When it boils briskly, lower the fire and simmer.

Variation

Add pre-cut *miyŏk* to boiling soup stock and add soy sauce to taste when it comes to a boil. This soup is very clear and light, whereas the other soup is thick and milky.

White Radish Soup   *Mu kuk,* 뭇국

Long Korean white radish makes good soybean paste soup *(toenjang kuk)* or clear soup seasoned with salt or soup soy sauce. The addition of oysters will make for a flavorful soup in the fall.

Radish Soup with Oysters   *Kul kuk,* 굴국

$\frac{1}{2}$ *long white radish* (**mu**)
1 cup oysters
3 cups anchovy soup stock
1 teaspoon sesame oil
1 teaspoon chopped garlic
1 teaspoon ginger juice
1 teaspoon soup soy sauce
1 teaspoon salt
a pinch of red pepper threads
 or shreds of dried red pepper

1. Cut white radish into strips. Sprinkle coarse salt on oysters (small ones preferable), remove pieces of shells, if there are any. Wash in cold water just once and strain.

2. Pour sesame oil in a heated pan and stir-fry radish strips with chopped garlic and ginger juice. Add anchovy soup stock, soup soy sauce *(kuk kanjang)* and salt.

3. When the radish is almost cooked, add oysters and bring to a quick boil. Add a pinch of red pepper threads or shreds of dried red pepper before removing from heat.

Oysters should be added right before serving and boiled quickly and briefly (about 1 or 2 minutes) because they will lose flavor and make the soup bitter if boiled a long time.

Egg Soup   *Kyeran t'ang,* 계란탕

$\frac{1}{4}$ cup ground beef
1 teaspoon sesame oil
1 teaspoon chopped garlic
2 tablespoons soaked and sliced oak mushrooms (**p'yogo**)
$\frac{1}{4}$ cup sliced green onion
3 cups water
1 egg

A. 1 teaspoon soy sauce
    $\frac{1}{2}$ teaspoon table salt

B. $\frac{1}{2}$ teaspoon sesame oil
   $\frac{1}{4}$ teaspoon table salt

1. Add sesame oil and chopped garlic to ground beef
   and stir-fry. Add sliced mushrooms.

2. Add water, season with (A) ingredients and bring
   to a boil. Add sliced green onion.

3. Blend egg with (B) ingredients. Pour in the
   boiling soup before removing from fire.

Meat Ball Soup   *Wanja t'ang,* 완자탕

1 cup lean ground beef
1 egg, beaten
flour, as needed
6 cups broth
$\frac{1}{2}$ cup sliced green onions

A. 1 teaspoon salt ($\frac{1}{2}$ teaspoon table salt)
    1 teaspoon soy sauce
    1 tablespoon finely chopped green onion
    $\frac{1}{2}$ teaspoon chopped garlic
    2 teaspoons sesame oil
    1 teaspoon sesame salt
    dash black pepper

B. 1 teaspoon soy sauce
    1 teaspoon table salt

1. Season ground beef with (A) ingredients
   and knead well.

2. Shape (1) into balls $\frac{1}{2}$ inch across. Roll each ball in flour and dip in egg.

3. Add (B) seasoning to the broth and bring to a boil. Add the meat balls and boil again. When the balls float to the top, add sliced green onion and remove from fire.

If you have beaten egg left, add it to the boiling broth.

Makes 8 servings.

Mung Bean Noodles and Beef Soup
Tangmyŏn soegogi kuk, 당면쇠고깃국

This is a good choice if you don't want to have the smell of seasoning on your hands that comes from shaping meatballs for Meatball Soup. It's quicker and simpler and the noodles make it milder.

1 cup ground beef
1 cup soaked mung bean (or potato) noodles
4 cups water or broth
$\frac{1}{2}$ cup sliced green onion

A. *1 teaspoon salt ($\frac{1}{2}$ teaspoon table salt)*
   1 teaspoon soy sauce
   1 tablespoon chopped green onion
   1 teaspoon chopped garlic
   1 teaspoon sesame oil
   1 teaspoon sesame salt
   1 egg

B. *$1\frac{1}{2}$ teaspoons soy sauce*
   $1\frac{1}{2}$ teaspoons salt

1. Mix beef with (A) ingredients.

2. Cut soaked mung bean noodles to 3-inch lengths.

3. Season water or broth with (B) ingredients and bring to a boil.

4. Mix an egg with the seasoned meat, add to the boiling broth by spoonfuls.

5. Add mung bean noodles. Cover and bring to a hard boil. When the noodles become transparent, add diagonally sliced green onion. Remove from fire.

45

Beef Stock Soup *Kom t'ang,* 곰탕

1 pound shank, brisket or ox tail (flank steak is nice
  but expensive)
16 cups water
1 white radish (the size of the meat will be enough)
2 teaspoons soup soy sauce (**kuk kanjang**)
1 teaspoon table salt

A. 1 tablespoon soup soy sauce (**kuk kanjang**)
    1 teaspoon black pepper
    1 tablespoon sesame oil
    1 tablespoon sesame salt
    1 tablespoon sliced green onion
    1 teaspoon chopped garlic

1. Boil meat in water, occasionally skimming off the froth.

2. Peel radish and cut into big chunks.

3. When the beef is cooked—poke it with a chopstick, it should not bleed—add radish. Simmer for about 3 hours until the water is reduced to about 8 cups.

4. Remove radish and beef. Season the soup with soup soy sauce and salt.

5. Cut radish into bite-size pieces. Thinly slice or shred the beef and mix with (A) ingredients.

6. Remove the layer of fat from the top of the broth. Pour the meat and vegetable mixture and radish back into the pot and bring to a boil.

This will make 8 servings. Soups that need a long time of boiling like this one taste much better when made in great quantities.

Dried Pollack Soup *Pugŏ kuk,* 북어국

1 dried and halved pollack (**pugŏ**)
  or 1 cup dried, shredded pollack strips
3 cups soup stock
1 green onion (enough to make ½ cup when cut)
1 or 2 teaspoons table salt
red pepper powder
black pepper

1. If unshredded, shred dried pollack to the length of your finger from the tip to the second knuckle; make 1 cup. Wash and drain.

2. Cut green onion the same size. Beat an egg. Blend pollack strips, green onion and beaten egg together.

3. Season soup stock with salt to taste and bring to a boil. Drop the pollack and egg mixture into the boiling soup by the spoonful. Add red pepper powder and black pepper to taste.

Variation 1
Stir-fry pollack strips with 2 teaspoons sesame oil and 1 teaspoon chopped garlic and add water. This method is faster but the pollack becomes chewy.

Variation 2
For a spicy variation, mix pollack strips, unwashed, with 1 tablespoon red bean paste *(koch'ujang)* and 1 tablespoon sesame oil. Let stand awhile. Add to the boiling broth. Add a beaten egg and green onion mixture before turning off the heat.

Spicy Beef Soup *Yukkaejang,* 육개장

A. 1 pound bones
   1 pound brisket
   20 cups water
   2 bundles green onions

B. 1 tablespoon chopped green onion
   $\frac{1}{2}$ tablespoon chopped garlic
   1 tablespoon red pepper paste
   1 teaspoon red pepper powder
   1 teaspoon soup soy sauce
   $\frac{1}{2}$ teaspoon salt
   $\frac{1}{2}$ teaspoon black pepper
   1 tablespoon sesame oil

2 tablespoons flour
1 egg

1. Bring bones and brisket to a boil over a high heat, skimming off the froth every now and then. Turn the heat down and simmer until the meat is tender. Remove the meat and bones when it is well cooked and shred into 2-inch-long strips.

2. Cut green onions in 3-inch lengths. Scald in the broth and then mix them with the shredded beef. Season with (B) ingredients. Sprinkle flour over the mixture.

3. Add the mixture to the broth and bring to a boil. Add a beaten egg. Salt the soup to taste. (Usually 3 cups soup will need 1 teaspoon soup soy sauce and $\frac{1}{2}$ teaspoon table salt.) Cover awhile before serving.

Boiled *kosari* (young shoots of bracken) or boiled taro stems are good to add.

Makes 6 servings.

Soybean Paste Soup *Toenjang kuk,* 된장국

Bean Sprout Soup
K'ongnamul kuk, 콩나물국

2 cups bean sprouts
3 cups broth
3 tablespoons bean paste (**toenjang**)
red pepper powder to taste

1. Clean the bean sprouts, cutting off the small root at the end of the stem. On second thought, perhaps you don't need to remove the roots for the latest finding is that they are loaded with asparagin acid which is supposed to do wonders for hangovers.

2. Mix soybean paste and broth. Add bean sprouts and bring to a boil. When you can smell the sprouts cooking, remove the lid and stir.

According to an old wives' tale, the smell peculiar to bean sprouts will linger if you open the pot before the sprouts are well cooked, but it does not hold when cooking with soybean paste.

I also like to season the soup with salt instead of soybean paste. Add some red peppers, and it really helps when you have a cold.

Radish Soup with Soybean Paste
Mu toenjang kuk, 무된장국

$\frac{1}{2}$ long Korean white radish (**mu**)
3 cups anchovy soup stock
3 tablespoons bean paste

1. Peel white radish and cut into 1-inch-thick circles. Cut the circles into 1-inch squares about $\frac{1}{2}$ inch thick. Or simply chop in any way to form thin slivers.

2. Season anchovy soup stock with bean paste: 1 tablespoon bean paste to 1 cup soup stock. Add radish slices and boil until the radish is tender.

3. If you prefer it spicy, add red pepper powder or red pepper paste when the soup is done.

Spinach Soup
Shigŭmch'i kuk, 시금칫국

1 bundle spinach
3 cups broth
3 tablespoons soybean paste

1. Trim and cut spinach in short lengths. Scald.

2. Add soybean paste to broth and scalded spinach. Bring to a boil.

Adding bean sprouts and clams makes it even better.

Korean Cabbage Soup
Paech'u kuk, 배춧국

1 Korean cabbage (paech'u)
3 cups beef broth
3 tablespoons soybean paste
2 teaspoons red pepper powder or 1 tablespoon red pepper paste
1 tablespoon chopped garlic
½ cup chopped green onion

1. Shred Korean cabbage into strips.

2. Season broth with soybean paste and add cabbage when it boils. Simmer until the cabbage is very tender.

   Keep in mind that cabbage shrivels to almost nothing when boiled. Put in more cabbage than you think you need and then add more. You need at least 3 to 4 cups shredded cabbage for 1 cup stock.

3. Add chopped garlic, chopped green onion and red pepper powder or red pepper paste when the soup is almost done.

Noodle and *Kimch'i* Soup
T'ŏllegi, 털레기

2 cups beef or anchovy (**myŏlch'i**) *stock*
$\frac{1}{2}$ *cup* kimch'i
2 ounces thin noodles or 1 cup sliced rice cake
(**ttŏkkuk ttŏk**)

1. Cut *kimch'i* into small pieces. (This is a nice way to get rid of left over *kimch'i*.) Mix *kimch'i* and broth in a cooking pot. (You can use either beef or anchovy broth. I find anchovy tastes better and is lighter.)

2. Boil thin noodles briefly and rinse in cold water. Drain.

   Or if you are using *ttŏk,* rinse the pieces in cold water.

3. Add noodles or *ttŏk* when the mixture is boiling. Serve when the noodles or *ttŏk* are cooked.

Because *kimch'i* is already seasoned, you don't need to add any seasoning. Adding slices of Spam is not a bad idea.

I hear this dish with a quaint name comes from Ch'ungch'ŏng-do Province. It is quite easy to fix when you can't think of anything else for lunch or when you crave something hot and spicy. Be sure to use enough broth lest it becomes gruel instead of noodle soup. Add another cup if you want it soupy.

Stew *Tchigae*, 찌개

There was a time when both soup *(kuk)* and stew *(tchigae)* were considered a must on a respectable dinner table. Some people still make it a point to have both at dinner. As for me, I make it a point to serve just one of the two. I would end up with a lot of leftovers if I served both.

Tchigae is usually saltier than *kuk*, but I try to make it not so salty and put in a lot of vegetables. I usually broil or boil something to go with the *tchigae*. Sometimes, when I feel there aren't enough side dishes, I think of adding a sautéed vegetable but end up not doing so because I know your father-in-law will say I am being extravagant. My *tchigae* has become a kind of compromise; it has a lot of liquid for a *tchigae*.

2 cups soup stock
2 tablespoons soybean paste (**toenjang**)
$\frac{1}{2}$ pack bean curd
4 ounces ($\frac{1}{2}$ cup) beef
$\frac{1}{2}$ onion
3 green peppers
2-3 soaked oak mushrooms (**p'yogo**) *(optional)*
$\frac{1}{2}$ zucchini *(optional)*
$\frac{1}{2}$ potato *(optional)*
$\frac{1}{3}$ cup green onion, cut diagonally
1 teaspoon chopped garlic
1 tablespoon salad oil

1. Cut the onion into 1-inch cubes, make $\frac{1}{3}$ cup.
   Cut mushrooms, zucchini and potato likewise, if
   you are using them. Remove the seeds from green
   peppers and cut in pieces smaller than the onion.
   Slice green onions diagonally.

2. Slice beef. Cut bean curd into cubes the size of the
   vegetables.

3. Heat a pan. Pour in salad oil and stir-fry the meat
   and chopped garlic. When the meat is cooked,
   add soybean paste and fry some more. Add
   onion, green pepper and soup stock. Bring to a
   boil and skim off froth. Add whatever vegetables
   you fancy. Add the bean curd. When it comes to
   a boil, throw in green onion and cover. Serve
   when it is piping hot.

Note

More vegetables can be added for a thicker stew.
Some people leave out the onions because they tend
to make the *tchigae* sweet but I always put them in
because I like their taste. Just remember that a
tchigae tastes better when cooked for a long time on
a low flame. If it is seasoned to suit your taste from
the start, it will become quite salty when cooked, so
make it bland at first. Also, it is better to add
soybean paste after the meat is cooked.

People seem to eat fewer vegetables in the United
States than in Korea. A *tchigae* with a lot of
vegetables is a good way to add vegetables to your
diet.

Pollack Stew
Tongt'ae tchigae, 동태찌개

$\frac{1}{2}$ long Korean white radish
$\frac{1}{3}$ cup green onion, sliced diagonally
1 tablespoon red pepper paste (**koch'ujang**)
2 teaspoons red pepper powder
1 teaspoon salt
1 bunch garland chrysanthemums (optional)

1. If frozen (most stores in the United States sell frozen fish), thaw pollacks in cold water, not in warm water because it will make the fish less flavorful and the meat mushy. Cut the pollack into 2-inch chunks, cutting across the body. It should make about 3 cups.

2. Cut white Korean radish into flat, rectangular pieces; make 1 cup. Slice the green onions diagonally; make $\frac{1}{3}$ cup.

3. Season beef stock with red pepper paste, red pepper powder, and salt. (Add beef slices now if you want to include them.) Add radish slices and bring to a boil. When the radish is almost cooked, add pollack. When the fish is cooked, add green onions and cover the pan. Remove from heat.

A handful of garland chrysanthemums added at the last minute enhances the flavor. Slices of bean curd can also be added. The *tchigae* becomes too thick when seasoned with red pepper paste only.

An addition of red pepper powder makes it quite refreshing. Soup soy sauce *(kuk kanjang)* can be used instead of salt but it tends to darken the *tchigae*.

Pollack Roe Stew
Myŏngnan chŏt tchigae, 명란젓찌개

$\frac{1}{2}$ *cup beef*
1 pair of salted pollack roe (**myŏngnan**)
$\frac{1}{2}$ *pack bean curd (about 1 cup)*
1 cup water
$\frac{1}{4}$ *cup green onion, cut diagonally*
1 tablespoon sesame oil
pickled shrimp juice (**saeu chŏt**) *to taste*

1. Slice beef. Cut pollack roe into 5 pieces if large and 3 pieces if small. Cut bean curd into $\frac{1}{2}$ inch cubes; make $\frac{1}{2}$ cup. Slice green onions diagonally.

2. Heat sesame oil in a pan and stir-fry the beef. Add water and roe and bring to a boil. Because the roe is already salty, it might not be necessary to add seasonings, but if it tastes bland, season with pickled shrimp juice (*saeu chŏt*). Add the bean curd and, when it comes to a boil, throw in the green onions and remove from the heat.

A couple of *myŏngnan* will be enough to make the *tchigae* in a small stoneware pot. The *myŏngnan* is much too expensive to think of buying it to make a *tchigae* but the recipe is worth trying when you already have some which is not of good quality or is stale.

Spicy Fish Stew *Maeunt'ang,* 매운탕

A. *1 catfish, red snapper, kingfish, cod or sea bass*
    Fresh fish is preferable, but frozen cod meat is
    quite all right.
    3 cups beef stock
    4 ounces (½ cup) beef (optional)
    ½ long Korean white radish
    ⅓ cup green onion, sliced diagonally
    1 bundle garland chrysanthemum (**ssukkat**)
    4 tablespoons **tadaegi**

B. *1 teaspoon chopped garlic*
    1 tablespoon red pepper powder
    1 tablespoon sesame oil
    2 teaspoons soy sauce
    1 tablespoon green pepper (optional)

1. Cut fish into 2-inch pieces, cutting across the body.

2. Cut white Korean radish into flat, rectangular pieces; make 1 cup. Slice the green onions diagonally; make ⅓ cup.

3. Make *tadaegi* seasoning by blending (B) ingredients to the thickness of cream. Chopped green pepper will enhance the flavor.

4. Season beef stock with *tadaegi*. (Add beef slices now if you want to include them.) Add radish slices and bring to a boil. When the radish is almost cooked, add fish. When the fish is cooked, add green onions and cover the pan. Remove from heat.

Maeunt'ang is cooked much the same way as pollack stew (*tongt'ae tchigae*). If using fresh fish, add thin slices of ginger to remove fishy odor. The *tadaegi* seasoning, which is best added from the start, will make it spicier and more savory but you need to keep it at a hard boil for a while to eliminate the garlic odor.

A. *12 to 15 pieces fried fish fillets (cod, pollack or any white fish)*

3 cups broth

4 ounces ($\frac{1}{2}$ cup) beef

$\frac{1}{2}$ cup long Korean white radish, sliced

1 tablespoon soy sauce

  or 2 tablespoons red pepper paste and 1 teaspoon table salt

  or 1 tablespoon red pepper powder and 1 tablespoon soy sauce

$\frac{1}{2}$ carrot

3 oak mushrooms (**p'yogo**) *soaked*

2 or 3 leaves Korean cabbage

1 medium size onion

B. *2 teaspoons chopped garlic*

1 tablespoon red pepper threads

1 teaspoon salt or 1 tablespoon soy sauce

1. Anchovy *(myŏlch'i)* stock is good enough if you have a large quantity of beef *chŏn* or fish *chon*, whereas beef stock is preferable if you have only a little. If you want the *tchigae* to taste like the fancy pot *(shinsŏllo)*, season it with soy sauce. If you want it to be spicy, use red pepper paste, red pepper powder and salt.

2. Slice beef. Slice radish into rectangular pieces *1* inch × *1$\frac{1}{2}$* inches. Cut carrot (and onion if you want to include it) to the same size. Shred Korean cabbage about the same size. Slice mushrooms.

3. Mix beef and radish with (B) ingredients. Layer the mixture on the bottom of the pan.

4. Add mushrooms, carrots, Korean cabbage and/or onions. Bring to a boil. Add the *chŏn* and bring to a second boil.

This is particularly nice to cook on the table. Serve when boiling hot.

Note

Chŏn (egg-coated, pan fried foods: see page 92) is already quite a dish to prepare in itself, so to make fresh *chŏn* specially for this *tchigae* is a bit too much work, to say the least. When you have leftover fish *chŏn*, however, this dish is a good alternative to having to heat up the *chŏn* meal after meal, and no one need know they are eating leftovers.

Kimch'i Stew *Kimch'i tchigae,* 김치찌개

3 cups **kimch'i**
8 ounces or 1 cup pork, beef or canned tuna
2 teaspoons chopped garlic
1 teaspoon crushed ginger
2 tablespoons cooking oil
1 tablespoon soy sauce
beef or anchovy broth to cover

1. Cut meat and *kimch'i* to 1-inch lengths.

2. Heat a pan. Fry chopped garlic and crushed ginger with oil. Add meat. When the meat is half cooked, add soy sauce. Stir-fry some more, and add *kimch'i.* Stir. Pour beef or anchovy (*myŏlch'i*) broth to cover the *kimch'i.* Bring to a boil and simmer for about 40 minutes.

When your *kimch'i* has gone sour or is simply not tasty, rinse it in water. Season the pork as you would to barbecue it, i.e. with *pulgogi* sauce, plus a generous amount of red pepper paste. Fry the pork and add the *kimch'i.* Pour in soup stock and boil.

If you want to use canned tuna instead of pork, fry the *kimch'i* first in salad oil. Drain the tuna well before adding it to the *kimch'i.* I add cut up potatoes when the *tchigae* boils. They are very good. I also add Chinese noodles (pre-soaked) when the *tchigae* is almost done.

You get a good *kimch'i tchigae* when the *kimch'i* is good. Using the same recipe, you can also make *kkaktugi tchigae.* I like it better when a fistful of dried anchovy is used instead of pork when frying the *kkaktugi.*

Soft Bean Curd Stew
Suntubu tchigae, 순두부찌개

3 cups soft bean curd (**suntubu**)
4 ounces ($\frac{1}{2}$ cup) beef
1 cup beef stock or water
$\frac{1}{2}$ cup **kimch'i**
$\frac{1}{2}$ cup shucked clams
3 stalks green onion
3 or 4 tablespoons salad oil
1 tablespoon red pepper powder
1 teaspoon chopped garlic
3 or 4 tablespoons sesame oil or perilla oil
pickled shrimp (**saeu chŏt**) *to taste*

1. Slice beef and *kimch'i* to $\frac{1}{4}$-inch pieces. Rinse and drain shucked clams. Slice green onion diagonally.

2. Pour salad oil in a pan over a low flame and fry red pepper powder. When the oil reddens, turn off the heat and strain to remove the pepper powder. The remainder is the red pepper oil *(koch'u kirŭm)*.

3. Stir-fry the beef and chopped garlic in sesame or perilla oil. Add the *kimch'i*. Add beef stock or water. When tasty, add soft bean curd. Boil some more and then add clams. When the clams have shrunk, season with pickled shrimp to taste and add the red pepper oil. Add the sliced green onions when the mixture is boiling hard, cover the pot and turn off the flame.

Unshelled corbicular clams (*moshi chogae*) may be added when the *tchigae* is boiling. They are cooked when the shells open up. Shelled shrimp is also a delicious addition.

To make bean curd at home

2 cups soybeans
16 cups water
3 tablespoons brine or 1 tablespoon Epsom salt mixed
with $\frac{1}{4}$ cup water

Soak soybeans in 5 or 6 cups of water for 6 to 8 hours. When the beans have softened, grind them with 16 cups of water in a blender.

Boil the liquid in a pot. When it begins to bubble, add a cup of cold water and bring to a second boil. Remove from the heat when it is bubbling. Pour the liquid into a cloth sack and squeeze to drain. (We use the liquid, not the dregs.)

Boil the bean liquid. Add brine when the liquid is hot and stir gently. The liquid will curdle and separate into curd and clear liquid. Leave it on a low flame for a while to allow the curd to harden.

You can serve it with *yangnyŏmjang* (See recipe on next page) or scoop it up with a perforated scoop and make bean curd *tchigae* with it.

If you find it too onerous to squeeze the hot liquid, squeeze before you boil it. Add brine only after you turn off the heat. The old wives' theory is that the bean liquid will yield less curd when squeezed cold, but a morsel more of bean curd is not really worth the effort. To be honest, squeezing the hot liquid is sheer torture.

Use a large pot to boil the bean liquid because it expands to about three times its size. A small pot will keep you really busy. It is a little easier and faster if you boil 6 cups of water first and add the bean liquid. If you do, you will have to grind the beans with 10 cups, instead of 16 cups.

You can buy brine at a grocery store or Epsom salt at a drug store. Epsom salt should be dissolved in water. Some say bean curd is very good for one's health and some say it is very bad. Japanese and Chinese eat it as much as Koreans and they are all doing quite all right, aren't they?

Bean Dregs Stew
Piji tchigae, 비지찌개

A. 1 cup soybeans
   10 ounces pork
   1 cup kimch'i
   1 cup soup stock

B. 2 tablespoons soy sauce
   1 teaspoon chopped garlic
   1 teaspoon ginger juice
   $\frac{1}{2}$ teaspoon black pepper

1. Soak soybeans in 3 cups of water for 5 to 6 hours until the beans swell to about 2 cups.

2. With pork, the fatty cuts are tender and delicious, but tenderloin or shoulder is not bad. Season sliced pork with (B) ingredients.

3. Cut *kimch'i* in $\frac{1}{4}$-inch lengths, enough to fill a cup.

4. Stir-fry the pork and the *kimch'i* together. Add soup stock and bring to a boil. Grind the swollen beans with 2 cups water in a blender and pour over the boiling pork and *kimch'i*. Don't stir. When it is cooked, mix it with the pork and *kimch'i*.

5. Serve the *tchigae* with a separate dish of *yangnyŏmjang* so that the diner can season it to his or her taste.

To make *yangnyŏmjang*

2 tablespoons soy sauce
2 tablespoons chopped green onion
1 teaspoon chopped garlic
1 tablespoon sesame oil
1 tablespoon sesame salt
1 tablespoon red pepper powder

Mix the ingredients. Chopped green peppers can be added.

Note

You can replace the pork with pork ribs or ham bones. Season them before cooking. Stir-fry them with *kimch'i*, and add water. When the meat is half cooked and the water has boiled down, add the ground beans. The *tchigae* tastes stronger and more flavorful when the pork or bones are seasoned with pickled shrimp juice (*saeu chŏt*). Be sure to blend the beans finely or you will end up with coarse dregs in your *tchigae*.

Young Cabbage Stew
Shiraegi tchigae, 시래기찌개

3 pound young Korean cabbage (**paech'u**)
3 cups soup stock
3 tablespoons anchovy powder
3 tablespoons soybean paste
1cup sliced green pepper
6 soaked oak mushrooms (**p'yogo**)
3 tablespoons chopped garlic
3 tablespoons cooking oil
3 tablespoons sesame oil

1. Scald young cabbage, rinse and drain by squeezing to make what is called *shiraegi*. Slice mushrooms, or if you have leftover mushroom stems, you can use them instead. Soak and slice them finely and add to the cabbage. Season with anchovy powder, soybean paste, sliced green pepper, garlic and oil. Knead and let stand for about an hour.

2. Stir-fry in a pan or *ttukpaegi* (earthenware pot). Add soup stock and simmer for 3 to 4 hours. When the stock has boiled down, add sesame oil.

Note

Shiraegi tchigae is simply delicious to eat with hot, freshly cooked rice. Adding wild onions (*tallae*) or Chinese chives (*puch'u*) is a good idea if you have them on hand.

You can also add some beef. Fatty pieces are better than lean.

Food Boiled or Fried in Sauce
Chorim, 조림 and *Pokkŭm*, 볶음

 A food delectably boiled in a soy sauce-based sauce (*chorim*) can make a great difference when your meal seems skimpy. For rice-loving Koreans for whom a meal is not a meal without a bowl of rice no matter how many sumptuous dishes they have, a good *chorim* or *pokkŭm* is quite irresistible.

A good sauce is of utmost importance for a good looking, appetite-whetting *chorim*. A well-cooked *chorim* is dark and glossy and, of course, never burnt. The material to be cooked should be put in the pan when the sauce is boiling. Water should be added two or three times to prevent burning. Lower the flame and simmer until thoroughly cooked. Turn up the flame and bring it to a quick boil one last time to achieve the gloss.

Fish Boiled in Sauce
Saengsŏn chorim, 생선조림

Any kind of fish (**saengsŏn**) *will do but fresh fish is preferable to frozen.*

1 pound fish
1 tablespoon vinegar
1 teaspoon salt
4 tablespoons fish chorim sauce (See page 28)
3 cloves of garlic
3 pieces ginger about the same size as garlic cloves
5 stalks of green onion

1. Rinse the cleaned fish in water mixed with vinegar. Drain, sprinkle lightly with salt and let stand for 30 to 40 minutes.

2. Slice garlic and ginger. Cut green onions diagonally or slice lengthwise after cutting them into 2-inch-long pieces.

3. Heat a frying pan. Pour oil into the pan and when it is hot, brown the fish on both sides. Ginger slices, added to the oil, will help eliminate the fish smell.

4. In another pan, make *chorim* sauce on page 28. When it boils, add garlic and green onion, bring to a boil again and add the fried fish. Simmer.

Note

Another way is to marinate a fresh fish in a mixture of soy sauce, cooking wine, and ground ginger for about 1 hour, then boil in the *chorim* sauce the same way.

Spoon the boiling sauce over the fish frequently to let the sauce seep into the fish. Cover the pan and simmer on a low flame at first. When the fish is almost cooked, remove the lid and boil vigorously on a high flame for a glazed, enticing look.

White radish chunks are very delicious when boiled together with the fish. Put them on the bottom of the pan under the fish, and be sure to add a little bit more soy sauce for the radish. Scalded Korean cabbage strips are also wonderful when cooked the same way.

Boiled Laver *Kim chorim,* 김조림

These recipes are particularly good if you have sheets of laver that have become discolored due to exposure to humid air or poor storage, but of course you can use good laver as well.

50 sheets of laver

To make sauce
   3 tablespoons soy sauce
   3 tablespoons sugar
   1 tablespoon red pepper paste (**koch'ujang**)
   1 tablespoon wine
   1 tablespoon sesame oil

1. Soak laver in water and rinse well. Drain.

2. Mix the ingredients to make sauce.

3. Bring the sauce to a boil and add the drained laver. Stir occasionally to keep from burning. Simmer for about 40 minutes; it's worth the effort because it will keep for a long time.

Flavored Laver *Kim much'im,* 김무침

10 sheets of laver

To make sauce
   1½ tablespoons soy sauce
   1½ tablespoons sugar
   1 tablespoon sesame oil
   1½ teaspoons red pepper paste

1. Shred the laver without roasting to about 1 inch.

2. Mix the ingredients and boil until well blended. Let cool.

3. Add shredded laver to the sauce, and mix well with your hand. The dish is ready when all the laver is covered with the sauce.

Browned and Boiled Bean Curd
Tubu chorim, 두부조림

1 pack formed bean curd (**tubu**)
1 teaspoon roasted salt (½ teaspoon table salt)
2 tablespoons oil for frying

To make **yangnyŏmjang** *sauce*
    2 tablespoons soy sauce
    1 teaspoon sugar
    1 teaspoon red pepper powder
    1 tablespoon sesame oil
    ½ teaspoon chopped garlic
    3 stalks green onions
    (3 tablespoons soup stock)

1. Cut the bean curd into rectangles 2 inches long, 1 inch wide and ½ inch thick. Lightly sprinkle with salt.

2. Slice green onions lengthwise to 2-inch lengths, or simply chop them. Mix them with other *yangnyŏmjang* ingredients. (I prefer not using any sugar.) This is enough when adding the sauce directly to the *tubu* pan but add 3 tablespoons soup stock if you want to boil the fried *tubu* and sauce in a new pan to make it softer and juicier.

3. Pour oil into a heated pan and brown both sides of the *tubu* pieces.

4. You can add the sauce and boil the *tubu* directly in the pan, or boil the sauce in another pan and add the browned *tubu* to it. The first way will make the *tubu* rather gummy whereas the second way will make it softer.

You can score the browned *tubu* and stuff it with seasoned ground beef before boiling it in the sauce, which involves more work but results in a more delicious dish. You may want to try it when you want to impress someone.

Beef Boiled in Soy Sauce
Changjorim, 장조림

1 pound brisket or shank
3 or 4 cups water
1 cup soy sauce
1 cup green peppers
1 tablespoon sugar
3 boiled eggs
6 to 8 cloves garlic

1. Cut beef into 2-inch chunks and soak in water for a while to bleed.

2. Peel garlic cloves. Remove stems from green peppers. (If Mexican peppers, 2 or 3 peppers will do.)

3. Boil water and put the beef in the boiling water. When the water begins to boil again, lower the flame and boil for about 30 minutes. Poke the meat with a skewer and if it does not bleed, add soy sauce and boil again. You can add sugar if you like it sweet.

4. Add green peppers. You might add whole boiled eggs, peeled in advance; they are very good when sliced and served separately or together with the meat. The meat is completely cooked when easily pierced with a skewer. Add garlic cloves and bring it to a boil again to allow the garlic to cook. Garlics cooked this way will not smell.

5. To serve, shred into small pieces if brisket and slice into thin pieces if shank.

Note

Changjorim was an effective way to preserve meat before the advent of refrigerators. It is still a very popular side dish, especially nice when you serve porridge. Because it is salty, it is served in a small amount.

Variations

Boil a shank of beef in water until it can be barely pierced with a skewer. Pour out some of the water (which you can use as soup stock or soup for *naengmyŏn* noodles), and add soy sauce, celery leaves, if available, whole black pepper corns and/or the green part of green onions. Boil until the meat can be easily pierced with a skewer. Remove the meat from the pan and cut in thin slices when cool. There you have delicious *pyŏnyuk* to eat dipped in vinegar soy sauce.

You can add the sliced meat to vegetables mixed with mustard sauce (*kyŏjach'ae*) to make something like the high priced *kyŏjach'ae* of Chinese restaurants. It is best to add a little bit of sugar when you boil the meat to make *kyŏjach'ae*.

1 pack formed bean curd (tubu)
1 teaspoon roasted salt ($\frac{1}{2}$ teaspoon table salt)
2 cups oil
3 tablespoons corn starch
1 egg

To make sweet sauce
    1 tablespoon soy sauce
    1 tablespoon sugar
    1 tablespoon wine
    1 tablespoon red pepper paste

1. Cut bean curd into $\frac{1}{2}$-inch cubes and lightly sprinkle with salt.

2. Beat an egg.

3. Coat the bean curd cubes with corn starch, dip in egg and fry. (The oil shouldn't be too hot lest they burn.)

4. Make sweet sauce by mixing the ingredients. Bring to a boil. (When you don't have red pepper paste, add another spoonful of soy sauce and spice it by adding 3 dried red peppers, shredded to about 1-inch pieces.)

5. Add the fried *tubu* to the sauce. Bring to a boil and simmer. Don't stir with a spoon but shake the pan.

Fried Anchovies
Myŏlch'i pokkŭm, 멸치볶음

1 cup dried anchovies
$\frac{1}{4}$ cup oil for frying

To make sauce
  1 tablespoon soy sauce
  $1\frac{1}{2}$ tablespoons sugar
  1 tablespoon cooking wine

1. Clean dried anchovies by removing heads and innards.

2. Fry anchovies on medium heat. Fry hard if you want the anchovies crunchy. Try to fry in as little oil as possible because you don't want to use the oil again because of the smell.

3. Boil ingredients to make sauce and add fried anchovies when the sauce is boiling. Mix.

Variation 1

If you prefer spicy anchovies, add red pepper paste and reduce the amount of soy sauce: $\frac{1}{2}$ tablespoon soy sauce, 1 tablespoon red pepper paste, 1 tablespoon sugar and 1 tablespoon wine.

Variation 2

Pour a generous amount of oil into a heated pan. Fry 2 teaspoons each of garlic and ginger slices in the oil, then add anchovies, then add 1 cup green peppers. When peppers are fried bright green, add original sauce and fry, stirring quickly to prevent burning. Add a drop of sesame oil when cooked. Put on a dish and sprinkle with 2 teaspoons of roasted sesame.

Note

The reason I use more sugar than soy sauce is because the anchovies are already quite salty.

You may want to save anchovy heads. Ground heads make a good addition to soups and stews.

Potatoes Boiled in Sauce
Kamja chorim, 감자조림

2 potatoes
4 tablespoons soy sauce
2 tablespoons sugar
1 tablespoon wine
½ teaspoon chopped garlic
½ cup water
1 tablespoon honey
1 or 2 green peppers
a dash of black pepper
½ teaspoon sesame oil
1 teaspoon whole roasted sesame seeds

1. Peel potatoes and cut into 1-inch cubes; make 2 cups. Soak the cubes for 20 minutes in salted water (2 teaspoons table salt to 1 cup water).

2. Seed green peppers and cut to the size of the potato cubes.

3. Make sauce by bringing soy sauce, sugar, wine, water and chopped garlic to a boil.

4. Add potato cubes when the sauce is bubbling. Don't stir but occasionally shake the pan. The potatoes are cooked when they can be easily pierced with a chopstick or a skewer. Add 1 tablespoon or less of honey. Add green pepper. Bring to a boil again, shaking the pan once or twice. When the sauce has boiled down, sprinkle with a dash of black pepper, sesame oil and whole roasted sesame seeds.

Button Mushrooms and Green Peppers in Sauce
Yangsong-i p'utkoch'u chorim, 양송이풋고추조림

4 cups button mushrooms
2 cups young, soft skinned green pepper
1 tablespoon sugar
3 tablespoons soy sauce
2 tablespoons cooking wine
a dash of pepper
2 teaspoons whole roasted sesame

1. Wash mushrooms and quarter them if large and halve them if small. Wash green peppers.

2. Boil sugar, soy sauce and wine. When the mixture is bubbling, add mushrooms. Add green peppers when the sauce has boiled down to half. Turn off the flame when cooked. Sprinkle with pepper and sesame before serving.

Note

If you prefer green peppers well cooked, add them right after mushrooms begin to boil. If you like them to remain bright green, wait until later. I discovered this dish at a temple where we had the 49th day memorial ceremony for Sujin's grandfather. They don't use garlic in temples but I sometimes add a little bit of chopped garlic. They don't use pepper or sesame either.

Mussels Braised in Sauce
Honghap chorim, 홍합조림

2 pounds unshelled mussels
$\frac{1}{4}$ teaspoon pepper
3 tablespoons soy sauce
2 tablespoons sugar
2 tablespoons rice wine or cooking wine
1 tablespoon sesame oil
1 teaspoon chopped garlic
1 teaspoon chopped ginger
(1 tablespoon pine nut powder)

1. Wash mussels well, removing hairy stuff from the shell.

2. Boil just enough water to cover the mussels. When boiling hard, add mussels. Remove from stove when the shells open. Take the mussels out of the shells and clean, removing brown, hairy stuff. Two pounds of mussels will yield about $1\frac{1}{2}$ cups when shelled and cleaned.

3. Sprinkle with pepper.

4. Boil soy sauce, sugar, wine, sesame oil, chopped garlic and chopped ginger. Add mussels when the mixture begins to boil. Simmer until the sauce has almost disappeared and then boil on high heat for a short while to glaze.

5. Place on a plate and sprinkle with chopped pine nuts, if available.

Note
Because cooking wine is sweeter than rice wine, less sugar should be added when using cooking wine.

It is better to soak and braise dried mussels but fresh ones are cheaper and easier to get. Removing the hairy stuff from the shells prior to cooking makes it simpler to clean the meat. Try to find shelled and frozen mussels. They are already cleaned and all you have to do is boil them in the sauce.

The water in which the unshelled mussels were boiled will make a very good seaweed soup (*miyŏk kuk*).

70

Black Beans in Sauce
K'ongjaban, 콩자반

1 cup black beans
1 cup water
4 tablespoons soy sauce
4 tablespoons sugar
4 tablespoons water

1. Wash black beans and boil in water. Boiling 10 minutes is enough to remove the strong odor of the half-cooked beans.

2. Boil soy sauce, sugar and 4 tablespoons of water in which beans were boiled. Add boiled beans and simmer on a medium flame. Do not cover. If covered, the mixture will boil over onto your range and also the beans will become mushy.

Fresh Squid Braised in Sauce
Mul ojing-ŏ chorim, 물오징어조림

2 fresh squids
3 tablespoons soy sauce
3 tablespoons sugar
1 tablespoon red pepper paste
2 tablespoons rice wine
1 tablespoon sesame oil
1 teaspoon chopped garlic
1 teaspoon chopped or sliced ginger

1. Clean and gut squids, cutting them down the middle. Cut legs to bite size. Remove skin from the opened squid. Score the inner side diagonally in a diamond pattern and cut to bite size. Two fresh squids will make a little more than 2 cups when cut up.

2. Boil the rest of the ingredients to make sauce. When the sauce begins to bubble, add squid pieces and boil on medium to high heat for 5 minutes.

Variation
Pork can make a nice addition. Cut pork the size of squid and boil in the sauce before adding the squid. Add 1 additional tablespoon of soy sauce for 1 cup of pork.

Braised and Steamed Food
Tchim, 찜

Tchim refers to seasoned and steamed food, but it can also mean many other things such as braised chicken (*tak tchim*) and braised ribs (*kalbi tchim*). Some *tchim* dishes are more like *chorim*, fried and braised in sauce, but dishes such as *kyeran tchim* (steamed egg batter) are really steamed.

Tchim dishes made with meat are quite different from foods that are stir-fried or boiled quickly. They entail a great deal more preparation and longer time to cook because the sauce requires plenty of time to thoroughly blend with the ingredients. On a dinner table, however, they make a difference worth every bit of your effort.

1 pound chicken
1 teaspoon chopped garlic
1 teaspoon chopped ginger
½ teaspoon salt or 1 tablespoon soy sauce
dash black pepper
1 tablespoon cooking wine
2 cups oil for frying
chorimjang *sauce (See page 28)*
½ cup water

1. Wings, drum sticks or tulips (wings turned inside out on the bones — perhaps you might be able to find them in the American market) are preferable but you can use a whole chicken, chopped into small pieces.
   Season with garlic, ginger, salt, black pepper and wine.

2. Deep-fry seasoned pieces in oil. If you don't like deep-frying, you can pan-fry them but do so in very hot oil because the soft chicken meat tends to break apart when cooking in sauce later.

3. Make *chorimjang* sauce for chicken on page 28. When the sauce boils, add the fried chicken and a little bit of water. Simmer.

If you want the meat firm, fry until the chicken is well cooked and simmer in sauce for a short while, just long enough to glaze the pieces. For extra glaze, you can dredge the chicken in starch before frying.

Chicken in Japanese Sauce
Teriyaki, 데리야키

3-pound chicken

To make sauce
   $\frac{1}{2}$ *cup soy sauce*
   2 tablespoons sugar
   6 tablespoons wine
   3 or 4 slices garlic
   3 or 4 slices ginger
   2 tablespoons roasted sesame seeds

1. Cut chicken to bite-size pieces and wash.

2. Make sauce by boiling the ingredients. It is quite convenient to keep some of the sauce on hand.

3. Place chicken in a pan and pour the sauce over it. The sauce should barely cover the chicken. Boil on high heat for 2-3 minutes, turning the pieces once or twice. Simmer on low. Chicken is cooked if it does not squirt when pricked with a skewer. Turn up the heat a little and stir quickly to glaze. Place on a plate and sprinkle with whole roasted sesame before serving.

You may add a little water to prevent chicken from sticking to the pan but you don't need to do so if the chicken was frozen. I find it most convenient to cook the chicken in a microwave oven for 20-30 minutes and then simmer on low heat but it has the disadvantage of running up the electric bill.

Chicken Slices *Tak p'yŏnyuk,* 닭편육

1 medium size chicken

A. *1 tablespoon soy sauce*
   $\frac{1}{4}$ *teaspoon black pepper*
   $\frac{1}{4}$ *teaspoon chopped ginger*
   $\frac{1}{4}$ *teaspoon chopped garlic*

B. *4 tablespoons soy sauce*
   1 tablespoon red pepper paste
   2 tablespoons sugar
   2 tablespoons honey
   4 tablespoons rice wine
   5-6 slices garlic, ginger

1. Debone chicken, working from the breast. (Be extra careful not to cut your finger!) Arrange loose meat lengthwise inside the skin and massage with a mixture of (A) ingredients. Bring the skin together and fasten with a skewer or toothpicks.

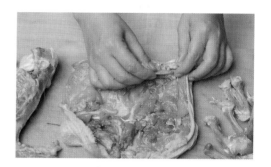

2. In a greased pan, brown the chicken on all sides.

3. Make sauce by boiling (B) ingredients. When the sauce boils, add the chicken and simmer, occasionally spooning the sauce over the chicken. Prick the chicken frequently with a skewer to prevent the skin from breaking as the chicken swells up as it cooks. If no liquid squirts out when pricked, add a little bit of water every now and then to prevent scorching.

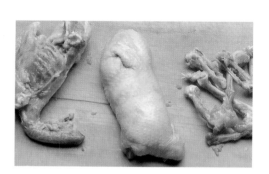

The chicken can be served hot, cut into thick slices and covered with the sauce, or cold, sliced like roast beef.

Note
When you cut up chicken, be sure to clean your knife and cutting board with scalding hot water and detergent because fresh chicken has germs that can cause food poisoning.

Chicken in Sauce *Yangnyŏm tak,* 양념닭

2 pounds of chicken wings, drumsticks or thighs
6 tablespoons soy sauce
1 tablespoon red pepper paste
5 tablespoons sugar
2 tablespoons tomato ketchup
2 tablespoons vinegar
1 teaspoon hot sauce
$\frac{1}{2}$ cup chopped onion
1 teaspoon chopped garlic
1 tablespoon chopped ginger
pepper to taste

1. If using thighs, score lengthwise. Season with soy sauce, pepper to taste, chopped garlic, and chopped ginger and let stand for 1 hour.

2. Brown the chicken pieces in a pan on both sides to remove fat. Drain the fatty oil. Add the rest of the ingredients and simmer. Some chicken meat is juicy and some not, so add water as needed. It is done when the chicken does not squirt when pricked with a skewer.

Note

You can substitute honey for the sugar, but I suggest you use honey and sugar together rather than honey only.

It should taste something similar to the *yangnyŏm t'ongdak* they sell in Seoul. My friends liked it so much that I bought some and worked out my own recipe. Try it and, if you think it does not taste right, by all means add other ingredients.

2 pounds spare ribs or back ribs
3 teaspoons soy sauce
1 teaspoon chopped garlic
1 teaspoon chopped ginger
$\frac{1}{4}$ *teaspoon pepper*
chorimjang *sauce (page 28)*
water
1 tablespoon pine nut powder

1. Spare ribs involve a lot of trimming but they are quite cheap, whereas back ribs are a little more costly but handier. (In Korea, there is no choice, there being no such distinction.) Score ribs at $\frac{1}{2}$ inch intervals, soak in cold water to bleed, and drain. Season with soy sauce, chopped garlic, chopped ginger and pepper. Let stand 15-20 minutes.

2. Pat ribs dry with kitchen towel and deep-fry.

3. Make the *chorimjang* sauce on page 28. When it boils, add the fried ribs. When the sauce returns to boiling, add 3 tablespoons of water. Repeat twice. Simmer on low heat. When the ribs are cooked, turn up the heat and boil to glaze them. Sprinkle with pine nut powder before serving.

Note

I suggest you fry a great many ribs and keep in small packs in the freezer to thaw and braise whenever you feel like having this dish.

If you don't like deep-frying, pan-fry, steam or roast in the oven for 25 minutes before boiling in sauce.

Short Rib Stew *Kalbi tchim,* 갈비찜

Short ribs have fat between the bones and meat. They are all right for soup stock but not very good for *kalbi tchim* because they lack flavor. English cuts have meat right next to the rib bones. The American supermarkets don't carry a great deal of them, just a few packages at a time. They are a little more expensive but it does not make much difference in the end because you don't have to do much trimming.

White Korean Radish
(Mu)

2 pounds ribs, cut into 2-inch lengths cooking foil
½ pound radish
*4 oak mushrooms (**p'yogo**)*
10 chestnuts
10 ginkgo nuts
1 egg

Oak Mushrooms
(P'yogo)

A. *½ cup grated onion*
   6 tablespoons soy sauce
   4 tablespoons sugar
   2 tablespoons honey
   3 tablespoons rice wine
   2 tablespoons sesame oil
   4 tablespoons chopped green onion
   1 tablespoon chopped garlic
   ½ teaspoon black pepper
   1 tablespoon sesame salt

Chestnuts *(Pam)*

Ginkgo Nuts
(Ŭnhaeng)

Short Rib Stew
Kalbi tchim

79

1. Mix (A) ingredients to make marinade.

2. Score the ribs at intervals of $\frac{1}{2}$ inch or less. Marinate in the marinade for 1 hour.

3. Separate eggs and beat. Fry the yolks and whites separately in very thin layers on a lightly greased pan. Cut into fine strips.

4. Cut white Korean radish into $2 \times 2 \times \frac{1}{2}$ inch pieces. Skin the ginkgo nuts and chestnuts. Soak mushrooms.

5. Wrap each rib with cooking foil, garnishing with pieces of radish, oak mushroom, chestnut, ginkgo nut, and strips of fried egg yolk, if you want to make it impressive (the strips don't enhance the taste but greatly improve the appearance). Don't close the foil tightly because it will be difficult to unwrap. Close it just tight enough to prevent juice from leaking. Add a spoonful of marinade before closing the foil.

6. Steam the wrapped meat in a steamer until the meat is done. If the meat is tough, it will take a long time to cook this way so test it carefully before removing from heat.

Variation 1

Scald the ribs in boiling water, and season with the sauce and simmer. Add green onions after the ribs are cooked. Sprinkle with sesame salt and sesame oil before serving.

Variation 2

If the ribs are not meaty, add brisket, cut the size of the ribs. Barely cover the meat and ribs with water and boil for 20-30 minutes. After skimming off the grease, pour in the marinade and simmer. Add radish pieces, oak mushrooms, chestnuts and/or ginkgo nuts at this time. They are very delicious.

Note

When you have many guests, it truly helps to have precooked ribs wrapped in cooking foil to warm up in the oven. Wrap individual portions of ribs with pieces of mushrooms and other ingredients. It tastes better if you sprinkle with chopped green onion before wrapping.

Braised Pork, Chinese Style
Toeji kogi tchim, 돼지고기찜

Pork belly meat *(samgyŏpsal)* is preferable but since it is fattening, try to get some that is not too fatty.

$1\frac{1}{2}$ *pounds pork*
3 or 4 tablespoons oil
3 or 4 tablespoons brown sugar
$\frac{1}{4}$ *cup soy sauce*
$\frac{1}{4}$ *cup wine*
2 cups water
6 or 7 green onions
7 or 8 oak mushrooms (**p'yogo**), *soaked*
about 5 slices of garlic and ginger
(8 to 10 Szechwan pepper corns)

1. Cut pork in pieces about 3 inches thick and wide.

2. Clean green onions. Cut at about 1 inch from the root and save the good white part at the center for other uses. Wash the roots and the leaves thoroughly.

3. Heat oil in a pan, add brown sugar. Fry pork on both sides until half cooked. Remove from heat and wash. So much fat will have been drained that your hands will not get greasy.

4. Rinse the pan if you want to use the same pan. Cook fried pork in a mixture of soy sauce, wine, green onion roots and leaves, garlic, ginger (stale ones are all right, because of the long cooking), and Szechwan pepper corns if you have them on hand. Start on medium heat. When the mixture starts boiling, reduce heat to low and simmer until meat becomes mushy tender.

5. Add soaked oak mushrooms when a skewer pierces the meat easily because by then the meat will have absorbed most of the seasoning. If mushrooms are added before this, they will absorb all the seasoning, becoming pickles, and the meat will remain bland.

You can serve hot or cold, cut like plain boiled pork.

Stewed Dry Pollack *Pugŏ tchim,* 북어찜

3 dried pollacks

A. *4 tablespoons soy sauce*
   1 tablespoon red pepper paste
   3 tablespoons sugar
   1 tablespoon sesame oil
   1 tablespoon cooking wine
   1 teaspoon chopped garlic
   1 teaspoon chopped ginger
   $\frac{1}{2}$ teaspoon black pepper
   $\frac{1}{4}$ cup sliced green onion

B. *1 teaspoon sesame oil*
   1 tablespoon roasted sesame

1. Soak pollacks in water. When softened, cut off the head, tail and fins. Cut in 2-inch pieces.

2. Make marinade by mixing (A) ingredients. (Green onions look the best when cut into 2-inch lengths and sliced thinly lengthwise.) Marinate pollack pieces in the sauce for 1 to 2 hours.

3. Grease a pan with salad oil and brown the pollack on both sides. Add $\frac{1}{2}$ cup water and simmer until the water has all evaporated (about 15 minutes). When done, add sesame oil and sprinkle with roasted sesame (B).

Note

If the pollack is not skinned, score the skin.
Half-dried pollack (*k'odari*) is just as good. You can also substitute thread thin strips of dried red pepper for the red pepper paste but be sure to add 1 tablespoon of soy sauce.

This is a favorite dish of elderly people. (There was a time when dried pollack cost more than beef.)

Save the head, bones and fins. They make good soup stock. You might also boil them for your dog. Dried pollack is to dogs what ginseng is to humans. If your dog gets sick, it is not a bad idea to feed it pollack soup before taking it to the veterinarian.

Egg Batter Steamed with Fish Roe
Al tchim, 알찜

3 eggs
½ cup sliced or minced beef
1 teaspoon soy sauce
pickled shrimp (**saeuchŏt**) *to taste*
  or pickled pollack roe (**myŏngnanchŏt**) *to taste*
2 tablespoons chopped green onion
1 teaspoon chopped garlic
¼ teaspoon black pepper

1. Break eggs and beat with a half shell of water for each egg.

2. Sprinkle meat with black pepper, season to taste with soy sauce and anchovy juice or pickled pollack roe. Add it to the eggs and beat again.

3. Pour mixture into a greased bowl or pan and steam.

This dish looked so delicious when I was small but it always went to a visitor or to my grandfather!

Note
You will regret it if you don't grease the bowl for the egg will stick to the bowl and never come off.

Steamed Egg Batter, Japanese Style
Kyeran tchim, 계란찜

2 eggs
1 cup anchovy stock (I find beef stock just as good)
6 medium size shrimp
½ cup beer
2 oak mushrooms (**p'yogo**), soaked
18 ginkgo nuts, if you have
1 tablespoon soy sauce
1 tablespoon cooking wine
salt to taste
sugar to taste

1. Sprinkle shrimp with salt and boil in water mixed with beer.

2. Season soaked mushrooms with a little bit of soy sauce and sugar. Lightly stir-fry ginkgo nuts and remove the inner skin.

3. Beat 2 eggs thoroughly. Add anchovy stock, soy sauce and cooking wine. Beat and pour through a sieve.

4. Place shrimp, mushrooms and ginkgo nuts in 6 greased cups and add sieved egg mixture. Steam. You might want to garnish with one or two green leaves such as the leaves of garland chrysanthemum (ssukkat).

Note

This is very soft and nice but it requires a lot of work. If you find the egg mixture too bland once you've added the seasoning, add salt. If you prefer it sweet, add sugar. Japanese seem to love sweet foods whereas Koreans don't.

Makes 6 servings.

Broiled Food *Kui,* 구이

Most Korean food is seasoned before broiling but it should not be done too far in advance. Broiled beef (*pulgogi*), for example, becomes bland and dull if seasoned longer than 1 or 2 hours. Broiling is best done over a charcoal grill. It not only enhances the taste of the meat but is also healthful because the grease will drain. How you broil makes a big difference even though you use the same seasoning. Whether you grill over charcoal or broil in a skillet or oven, don't turn the meat over until one side is completely cooked. Turning it again and again is a sure way to make it tasteless.

Grilled or Broiled Beef
Soegogi kui, 쇠고기구이, or Pulgogi, 불고기

1 pound beef
pulgogi *sauce (see page 27)*

1. If it is not already sliced, cut about $\frac{1}{4}$ inch thick if tenderloin. If sirloin, cut about $\frac{1}{8}$ inch. (I like it a little thicker than ordinary *pulgogi* slices.) Score both sides.

2. Make *pulgogi* sauce on page 27.

3. Place a layer of beef in a pan, sprinkle with the sauce, add another layer, sprinkle again, and repeat. A TV chef says it tastes better if you knead the meat with sauce until it gets sticky. I tried and perhaps it did taste a little better, I can't say for sure. What is important is to have good meat in the first place.

4. Grill or broil.

Note
If the meat is tough, marinate it in a mixture of ground onion, honey and wine for several hours before seasoning. Remember to put that much less honey when you make the *pulgogi* sauce.

If you like your meat thin in the traditional *pulgogi* fashion, ask your butcher "to slice the beef like bacon." I tried and got meat sliced like that in a Korean butcher shop. You can get *pulgogi* meat in Korean or Japanese grocery stores, but they are not always nearby.

If you have glutinous rice powder or buckwheat powder, dredge seasoned meat in it and fry in a greased pan. It is delicious if you wrap it around slices of green onions and fresh perilla leaves (*kkaennip*) mixed with fresh vegetable sauce (see page 29).

Broiled Beef Sanjŏk 산적

1 pound tenderloin
pulgogi *sauce (page 27)*
1 tablespoon pine nut powder

1. Cut beef twice the size of your palm and a little thinner than steak. Score deeply at $\frac{1}{8}$ inch intervals on both sides so that it will absorb the marinade.

2. Season with *pulgogi* sauce and let stand for a couple of hours for the sauce to absorb. When you broil, remember to turn just once because turning it will shake the sauce off the meat.

3. Cut across the scores into bite-size pieces and serve. It will look and taste better when sprinkled with pine nut powder.

Broiled Pork
Toeji kogi kui, 돼지고기구이

1 pound pork (I wouldn't buy tenderloin for this recipe because it is too lean. Roast would be better.)
2 tablespoons soy sauce
2 tablespoons red pepper paste
2 tablespoons wine
3 tablespoons sugar
1 tablespoon sesame oil
1 tablespoon sesame salt
2 tablespoons chopped green onion
1 teaspoon chopped garlic
1 teaspoon chopped ginger
$\frac{1}{4}$ teaspoon black pepper

1. Slice pork like you would for *pulgogi* and score lightly.

2. Mix the ingredients to make seasoning sauce. If you are using tenderloin, add a tablespoon of salad oil to soften the meat.

3. Season the meat layer by layer. If you prefer spicy meat, add more red pepper paste, but take out an equal amount of soy sauce.

4. Broil or pan-fry, making sure the meat is completely cooked.

Broiled Pork Ribs
Toeji kalbi kui , 돼지갈비구이

3 pounds back or spare ribs

A. *2 tablespoons soy sauce*
   1 teaspoon chopped garlic
   1 teaspoon chopped ginger
   dash black pepper

B. *4 tablespoons soy sauce*
   4 tablespoons red pepper paste
   4 tablespoons wine
   6 tablespoons sugar
   2 tablespoons sesame oil
   2 tablespoons sesame salt
   4 tablespoons chopped green onion
   2 teaspoons chopped garlic
   2 teaspoons chopped ginger
   $\frac{1}{4}$ teaspoon black pepper

1. Massage pork ribs with a mixture of (A) ingredients. Let stand for about 30 minutes.

2. Broil in oven for 40-50 minutes at 350° F. A lot of fat will have drained and the meat will be almost cooked.

3. Separate the ribs and score, brush with the sauce (*yangnyŏmjang*) made of (B) ingredients and broil again briefly.

This recipe involves a lot of work but it is worth it.

You will notice the sauce is the same as the one for the broiled pork on the previous page. Because of the bones, however, you will need only two-thirds as much of the sauce as you need for the broiled pork.

2 pounds L.A. cut or English cut of beef ribs
½ cup grated onion
2 tablespoons honey
pulgogi *sauce (page 27)*

1. For English cut ribs, soak in water to bleed thoroughly. You don't have to do so with L.A. cuts.

2. Trim fat from ribs and score. For English cut ribs, score down to the bones so that when the ribs are broiled, the bones can be easily removed. Scoring at ½-inch intervals will make them convenient to eat.

3. Marinate in a mixture of grated onion and honey. After 2 to 3 hours, season with *pulgogi* sauce. Because ribs taste better when sweet, you don't need to subtract from the sauce the amount of sugar or honey that went into the marinade unless you used a lot.

4. Broiled ribs are as greasy as they are tasty. When broiling, adjust the grill high above the fire and let as much fat drain as possible. Grill over charcoal whenever possible. It tastes much better.

Beef Pot Roast
Soegogi naembi kui, 쇠고기냄비구이

4 pounds sirloin
1 tablespoon garlic powder
1 tablespoon salt
  or 1½ tablespoons garlic salt

1. Sprinkle roast with garlic powder and salt or garlic salt.

2. Place it in a pot with a three-ply bottom or a Dutch oven, without water, and roast on medium to low heat. Roast is more tasty when the inside is cooked to medium but if you prefer it well done, cook it longer. It takes about 1 and a half hours to roast 4 pounds. Turn off the heat if juice oozes when poked with a skewer. It will keep cooking even after you turn off the heat.

3. After the meat is cooled, cut into thin slices.

Make salad with perilla leaves (*kkaennip*), lettuce, green onion, radish sprouts and whatever other vegetables you have with a mixture of equal amounts of soy sauce, vinegar and sugar and a little sesame salt and red pepper powder. It is quite refreshing to have the vegetables wrapped with sliced roast.

Salt Roast
Soegogi sogŭm kui, 쇠고기소금구이

7 pounds beef sirloin or tenderloin
8 cups salt (do not use table salt)
1 egg yolk

Mix salt with the egg yolk. Paste the mixture on the roast thick enough to completely cover the meat. Roast in oven about 2 and a half hours at 350° F. Remove from oven 20 minutes after turning off the heat. Crack the salt off. Cut to a generous thickness and serve on a plate.

Note

This is good served with baked potatoes, rolls, carrots braised in butter or other braised vegetables. I like to dip it in seasoned vinegar soy sauce. A bowl of *kimch'i* makes it even more delicious.

Broiled Fish *Saengsŏn kui,* 생선구이

1 pound fish
(Any fish will do, but if frozen, thaw in the
refrigerator if possible.)
1 tablespoon rough salt

Clean the fish, removing innards and scales. Cut diagonal slits on both sides. Salt it with rough salt and let stand for awhile. Wash in the salt water in which forms from the salted fish and broil.

I place a wooden chopstick on the grill and broil the fish on it so that the skin does not stick to the grill. The grill should be kept as high above the fire as possible.

Variation 1

Mix soy sauce and sugar (2 spoons soy sauce to 1 spoon sugar) and boil until the sugar melts. Brush the mixture on the broiled fish and serve. It tastes more interesting than plain broiled salted fish.

Variation 2

For 1 pound fish, mix 2 tablespoons soy sauce, 2 tablespoons sugar, 1 tablespoon cooking wine, 5 slices each of ginger and garlic. Boil until the sugar melts. Marinate a cleaned fish in the mixture for about 1 hour and broil.

You can also make a nice stew (*tchigae*) with fish broiled like this. Slice beef into thin slivers and season with chopped green onions, garlic, pepper, and sesame oil. Layer sliced carrots, green peppers, *minari* (This vegetable is similar to watercress, which can be found in American supermarkets, Korean parsley or drop wort, but it doesn't seem to have a proper English name, so we will just call it *minari*.), mungbean sprouts (*sukchu*) and/or mushrooms in a low stew pot and top with the seasoned meat and broiled fish. Add beef stock, cover, and boil.

Variation 3

Add red pepper powder and sesame salt to the marinade of Variation 2. Spoon it over the broiled fish and serve. The fish will taste like it was braised (*chorim*).

Note

It isn't a big deal if broiled salted fish is a little too salty but when you are going to add sauce (in Variation 1), be sure to salt the fish very lightly in the first place.

I put a few drops of vinegar in the water when I wash fish. It eliminates the fishy smell.

Pan-Fried Foods *Chŏnya*, 저냐

Chŏnya, foods coated in flour and egg and pan-fried, can be made with any number of things such as fish fillets, vegetables and meat patties. The ingredients are first dredged in flour, then dipped in egg and finally fried in just enough oil to grease the pan. The frying pan should be preheated before the oil is poured in. It is important to fry slowly on low heat and to turn only once. If high heat is used, the outside of the *chŏnya* will burn and the inside will remain uncooked. If turned over and over while frying, it will look tattered. When frying salted ingredients, such as meat patties (*kogi chŏn*), the pan should be cleaned with a paper towel or water between each batch for neat-looking *chŏnya*.

When preparing the egg batter, add salt before beating and let it stand for awhile so that it will be a bright color and coat more evenly. Be careful not to use too much flour for it will rob the food of flavor. The flour is to help the egg coating stay put. *Chŏnya* do not need to be served piping hot. Let drain on a bamboo tray or paper towel for awhile before arranging them on a serving dish.

Some people prefer not to wash their frying pan every time they use it, saying things stick to the pan if it is washed frequently, but I make it a point to clean it with a paper towel and then wash it in soapy water. If it is washed, the odor of the oil will not linger and the pan will always look like new. Clean not only the inside but the outside of the pan as well. The pan will become sticky and greasy in no time if you do not clean it after each use. You will find cooking much more pleasant if you keep your pots and pans bright and shiny. Also, you will be able to train yourself to use a minimum number of pots and pans so you won't have to go to the trouble of washing them.

When using a Teflon-coated pan, use Teflon, plastic, or bamboo utensils to protect the coating and keep it from flaking. You do not want to cause flaking, because Teflon, which is harmful if ingested, could get into the food. It makes me quite nervous when metal cooking utensils are used in TV cooking classes.

Pan-Fried Slices of Beef
Kogi chŏn, 고기전

1 pound beef
2 eggs
3 tablespoons flour
½ teaspoon table salt
dash pepper
3 tablespoons cooking oil

Vinegar soy sauce
　　1 tablespoon soy sauce
　　2 teaspoons vinegar
　　½ teaspoon sugar

1. Slice beef as you would for making *pulgogi* or ask your butcher to slice it like bacon. If you want to slice the beef yourself, tenderloin is the easiest.

2. Score beef slices across the grain and sprinkle with salt and pepper.

3. Beat eggs with a dash of salt, let stand.

4. Dredge beef in flour, dip in egg and fry in a pan. Serve with vinegar soy sauce.

Variation
Before dredging in flour and dipping in egg, season the sliced beef with *pulgogi* sauce, using about half the amount you would to season *pulgogi*. Reduce sugar when making the sauce if you do not want the meat to taste too sweet.

Meat Patties
Wanja chŏn, 완자전 or *Ton chŏn ,* 돈전

1 pound minced beef
*½ cup bean curd (**tubu**), crushed*
½ cup chopped onion
1 teaspoon salt
1 teaspoon chopped garlic
2 teaspoons sugar
1 tablespoon sesame oil
½ teaspoon black pepper
1 tablespoon sesame salt
3 tablespoons flour
2 eggs

1. Crush the *tubu* with the side of a knife on a chopping board and squeeze in a piece of cloth to drain.

2. To the minced beef, add *tubu*, diced onion, and seasonings. Knead well.

3. Shape the mixture into bite-size patties, dredge in flour, coat with beaten egg and fry.

Turn once and once only. If you turn them over and over, the juice that comes out will burn and stick to the patties, leaving dark, unsightly spots on them.

The patties will not be coated sufficiently if you remove them from the egg with chopsticks. Spoon them up with a bit of the egg in the spoon to make neat, golden patties.

Pan-fried Fish Fillet, Zucchini and Meat Patties
Saengsŏn chŏn, Hobak chŏn and Ton chŏn

95

Pan-Fried Fish Fillet
Saengsŏn chŏn, 생선전

1 pound fish fillets (flounder, croaker, red snapper, cod, pollack or any white fish)
2 teaspoons table salt
1 cup water
$\frac{1}{4}$ teaspoon black pepper
$\frac{1}{2}$ tablespoon fresh red pepper, chopped
1 tablespoon green pepper or bell pepper, chopped
2 tablespoons flour
2 eggs

1. Mix water and salt and soak fish fillets for 5 minutes. Drain well and sprinkle with pepper.

2. Beat eggs.

3. Finely chop red pepper and green pepper. Rinse in water, drain, sprinkle with salt and mix in eggs.

4. Dredge fish pieces in flour and dip in the egg. Pour oil in a heated frying pan and cook the egg-coated fish. When the pieces are cooked a little, spoon some of the chopped pepper from the egg on them and turn. The fish is done by the time the egg is cooked.

I add the chopped pepper for decoration and also to enhance the taste. I make it a point to do so especially when I use frozen fish because frozen fish is definitely less savory than fresh ones. I find frozen fish tastes better if it is first coated with sesame oil and then sprinkled with salt and pepper.

Pan-Fried Green Onion P'a chŏn, 파전

2 bundles thin green onions
$\frac{1}{2}$ cup sliced beef
$\frac{1}{4}$ cup clams
$\frac{1}{4}$ cup sliced squid
$\frac{1}{4}$ cup chopped shrimp
$\frac{1}{4}$ cup crab meat
3 eggs
3 tablespoons flour

A. $\frac{1}{2}$ tablespoon soy sauce
   1 teaspoon sugar
   $\frac{1}{2}$ teaspoon salt
   $\frac{1}{2}$ tablespoon chopped green onion
   1 teaspoon chopped garlic
   $\frac{1}{2}$ teaspoon sesame oil
   dash pepper
   1 tablespoon sesame salt

1. Clean green onions and quarter lengthwise if thick and halve if thin. When making small *p'a chŏn*, about palm size, cut the green onions into 2-inch lengths; we need about 4 cups. To make large plate-size *p'a chŏn*, cut the onions in the middle or a little shorter than the diameter of the plate. The ingredients are enough to make 2 plate-size *p'a chŏn*.

2. Season meat with (A) ingredients.

3. Squid and/or any kind of shellfish can be added. Shell and devein shrimp. Remove the skin from the squid and cut into fine slices.
Cut shellfish into small pieces.

4-A. To make small *p'a chŏn*, mix green onion pieces and seasoned beef, adding whatever shellfish you have. Season the mixture with salt. Sprinkle with flour and mix with egg. Spoon the mixture into disk shapes in a heated pan and fry.

4-B. For making large *p'a chŏn*, beat eggs. Sprinkle flour over pieces of green onion and mix them with half of the beaten egg. Spread the mixture on a heated, oiled pan, place the seasoned meat and shellfish between the green onion, then cover with the rest of the egg. Lower heat to let the ingredients cook. Turn when one side is well cooked.

Note

Glutinous rice powder is added to the egg in Tongnae *p'a chŏn*, the hefty, large *p'a chŏn* originating in Tongnae, but I think egg alone is good enough. Celery, cut the length of the green onion, may also be added.

Keep in mind that the *p'a chŏn* is to be dipped in a vinegar and soy sauce mixture at the table, so don't make it salty. Soy sauce is necessary for seasoning the minced beef, however, because it helps eliminate the meat odor. Don't add salt to the crab meat because it is already salty enough. In general, salting the egg and the green onion is enough.

P'a chŏn, Simpler Version

Thin green onions, flour, eggs

Cut green onions in the middle. Halve the bulbous white stalks lengthwise and beat (don't cut) them flat with the back of the knife. Mix the white and green pieces together and sprinkle with flour. Dip into egg beaten with salt and fry in a heated pan. Serve with a sauce of vinegar and soy sauce.

Note

P'a chŏn without other ingredients such as meat or shellfish is favored by people who like the flavor of green onion. Young spring onions make especially flavorful, fresh-tasting *chŏn*. You can also make good *chŏn* with the stems of *minari* the same way.

Mung Bean Pancake *Pindaettŏk,* 빈대떡

1 cup skinned mung beans
1 cup water
$\frac{1}{2}$ teaspoon salt ($\frac{1}{4}$ teaspoon table salt)
$\frac{1}{2}$ cup ($\frac{1}{2}$ pound) beef or pork (tenderloin)

A. 1 teaspoon soy sauce
   1 teaspoon sesame oil
   1 teaspoon chopped garlic
   1 teaspoon ginger juice
   1 cup thin green onion

   $\frac{1}{2}$ cup sliced onion
   $\frac{1}{2}$ cup mung bean sprouts
   4 ounces oyster mushrooms (**nŭt'ari**)
   1 cup **kimch'i**
   1 teaspoon sesame oil

B. 1 teaspoon garlic
   1 teaspoon ginger
   1 tablespoon sesame oil
   1 tablespoon sesame salt
   $\frac{1}{2}$ teaspoon pepper
   $\frac{1}{2}$ teaspoon salt

1. Wash and soak 1 cup skinned mung beans in water for about a day at room temperature, or about two days in the refrigerator. One cup dried mung beans will become 2 cups when well soaked.

2. Cut meat into thin strips and season with (A) ingredients.

3. Cut *kimch'i* into thin strips and squeeze juice out (Not too much lest the *kimch'i* become tasteless!). You should have about $\frac{1}{2}$ cup of *kimch'i* after squeezing. Mix with 1 teaspoon sesame oil.

4. Cut green onion into 2-inch-long pieces. Slice onion into thin strips. Wash mung bean sprouts. Scald mushrooms, squeeze and sprinkle with a little salt.

5. To the seasoned meat, add *kimch'i*, green onion, onion, mushrooms and season with (B) ingredients.

6. Add 1 cup water to soaked mung beans and grind in a blender to make a thick batter. Add $\frac{1}{2}$ teaspoon salt, but not if the seasoned ingredients are already salty. Put all of the seasoned ingredients into the mung bean batter and mix well. I can't really say how much salt should be added because it depends on how salty the *kimch'i* is or how much *kimch'i* you want to add. The best way is to fry a piece and taste it before you add any more salt.

7. Drop the batter by spoonfuls onto a hot, oiled pan. Place 4 or 5 bean sprouts on each mung bean circle. (If you find this way troublesome, mix the entire sprouts with the batter at the last minute.) Fry until golden brown and turn once.

Note

When *kimch'i* is not available, salted bellflower roots will do. Dried young shoots of bracken (*kosari*), soaked in water until tender, are also good additions. But simple *pindaettŏk* made of only ground mung bean is also nice. My mother loved it so much that I used to fry several pieces for her before adding other ingredients. I make a point to make *pindaettŏk* that way when I prepare food offerings for her memorial service.

Pindaettŏk tastes better when fried in oil in which beef or chicken has been fried than in new oil. Sometimes I fry pork fat in a frying pan until the fat fries out and then I grind it with the mung beans. It makes the *pindaettŏk* more savory.

If you can, get skinned mung beans in the first place. Removing the skins from the soaked beans yourself can be quite tiresome. A tip from your aunt in Champaign: Soak beans in water in the refrigerator for 3 or 4 days before grinding. I tried it and the *pindaettŏk* was more tender.

Although most people prefer pork in *pindaettŏk*, I sometimes use choice cuts of beef because it tastes better to me.

99

Eggplant, potato, zucchini, carrot, green peppers, onion
1 cup flour
1 cup water
1 tablespoon salt

1. Add water and salt to flour. Mix well.

2. Cut the potato into $\frac{1}{8}$-inch-thick slices, dredge in flour, dip in the paste and fry in a heated, oiled pan.

3. Fry the eggplant and zucchini the same way.

You might want to slice the leftover pieces of the potato, eggplant and zucchini into thin strips and mix them with strips of green peppers, carrots and onions. Add an egg to the paste. Dip the vegetables in it and fry the same way.

Note

I do not salt the vegetables because salt will make them tough. Besides, it will make the vegetables sweat, which in turn will make too much flour stick to them. The end result: the *chŏnya* will be as hard as stale biscuits.

Check if the potato *chŏnya* are completely cooked by pressing them with a spoon. The eggplant is cooked if the flour paste is cooked and the zucchini if it has turned bright green. I learned this recipe at the Buddhist temple where we had the memorial service for Sujin's grandfather on the 49th day after his death, and they were good!

You can spread the beef mixture of *wanja chŏn* on the zucchini pieces and fry the same way, dredged in flour and dipped in beaten egg. Or fry the zucchini pieces in oil without any addition. Sprinkle with *yangnyŏmjang* sauce and serve.

To make *yangnyŏmjang*

1 tablespoon soy sauce
$\frac{1}{2}$ *teaspoon sugar*
$\frac{1}{4}$ *teaspoon vinegar*
1 teaspoon red pepper powder
2 teaspoons chopped green onion
2 teaspoons sesame salt
1 teaspoon sesame oil

Eggplant *(Kaji)*

Green Pepper
(P'utkoch'u)

Fried Oyster Mushrooms and Bell Pepper
Nŭt'ari Piman chŏn, 느타리피망전

14 ounces oyster mushrooms (**nŭt'ari**)
3 bell peppers
¼ cup sliced onion
2 tablespoons powdered coffee creamer
1 egg
½ teaspoon salt

Oyster Mushroom
(*Nŭt'ari*)

1. Blanch mushrooms in salted, boiling water, rinse and squeeze gently. They will become about a cupful. Shred.

2. Cut bell peppers the same size as the shredded mushrooms, slice onions.

Chinese Chives
(*Puch'u*)

3. Mix the three with the creamer. Beat an egg with salt. Mix all together. Fry by the spoonful in a heated pan.

Note

The powdered creamer works as a tenderizer. I have made this dish frequently ever since I first discovered it at a wedding dinner. It is tasty and easy to make. Besides, oyster mushrooms (*nŭt'ari*) are sometimes outrageously cheap. But I expect they are quite expensive in the States. What a shame, because they are so cheap at Seoul's Karak Wholesale Market!

Zucchini
(*Hobak*)

Speaking of mushrooms, fried oak mushrooms (*p'yogo*) are also very delicious and easy to prepare. Remove the stems, brush on sesame oil and salt, and fry in a greased pan. They are especially good for those who are worried about cholesterol.

Minari

Crab Meat Patties *Kyesal chŏn,* 게살전

2 cups crab meat (canned or removed from cooked crabs)
2 eggs
1 cup green onion

Cut green onion into pieces 2-inches long and slice lengthwise. Mix with crab in beaten egg. Fry by the spoonful in a heated pan. Serve hot with vinegar and soy sauce for dipping.

Note

This is very easy to make and liked by everyone. Its only drawback is that it is rather expensive. Be sure to slice green onion finely. If you have red peppers on hand, add some, chopped or sliced. They make it prettier. You don't need to add salt because crab meat is already salty enough.

Potato Pancake *Kamja chŏn,* 감자전

1 or 2 potatoes, to make 1 cup when grated
½ teaspoon table salt
dash black pepper
½ cup vegetables (onion, green onion, perilla leaves, green pepper, and/or Chinese chives)

1. Peel the potatoes, removing the eyes, and soak in water.

2. Slice onion into thin strips.

3. Cut green onions, perilla leaves (*kaennip*), green pepper and Chinese chives into 2-inch-long strips.

4. Grate the potato, add salt and black pepper.

5. Mix potato starch with sliced vegetables and add to grated potato.

6. Heat a pan, pour a little oil and drop the potato batter by the spoonful. Fry until both sides become golden brown.

7. Serve with vinegar soy sauce sprinkled with chopped green pepper.

Makes about 12 pancakes.

Note

You do not need all of the vegetables listed. Any number of them will do. Or you can fry the potato alone, in which case you should halve the salt.

Instead of mixing the vegetables and grated potato, you could drop the potato first and add onion slices and chopped red pepper while it is cooking.

Vegetables become tough if salt is added to them; add salt to the potato only. Potato tends to discolor if left in the air for a long time. Add salt immediately.

For children who do not like onions, you could grate them and add to the potato batter.

Rice Porridge *Chuk,* 죽

Long ago when food was scarce, people ate *pap* (rice), cooked with or without other grains, in the morning and *chuk*, rice porridge, in the evening because, for the poor, *chuk* was a way to stretch what little grain they had, especially if they added vegetables and plant roots to it. Apart from saving grain, the combination of *pap* for breakfast and *chuk* for supper seems to me to be a reasonable diet that does away with any worries about getting fat because one would burn up all the calories from the breakfast during the day while taking in few calories with the *chuk* in the evening. Nowadays, however, a great many people have *chuk* for breakfast because it is simple to make and eat. I can think of nothing better than *chuk* for the sick, especially for those who don't have an appetite. It is also ideal for snacks, especially at night.

Most people tend to think all one has to do to make *chuk* is to dump rice into a great quantity of water and boil it, but this only makes boiled rice water, not *chuk*. Follow the measurements given here to get the right thickness. Be sure to cook on low heat, otherwise the rice will not swell completely and all the water will boil away before the rice is cooked.

Rice Porridge *Hüin chuk,* 흰죽

1 cup rice (soaked)
2 teaspoons sesame oil
4 cups water

1. Soak rice in water for 1 hour, drain well.

2. Drop sesame oil in a pan and stir-fry rice for 4 to 5 minutes. Add 4 cups of water and bring to a boil. When it begins to bubble up, stir once. Turn heat to the lowest and cover. Simmer. The *chuk* is done if the rice grains have become translucent and the water is absorbed.

We do not salt *chuk* because it is usually served with soy sauce or pickles.

Variation

Grind the soaked rice with sesame oil in a blender. Pass through a sieve. Boil the thin rice water on the top first and add the sediment in the bottom. Simmer.

Add some Chinese leeks when you cook *hüin chuk* ; it is very comforting when you have stomach trouble in summer. It is also good for a baby's stomachache if you season it with pickled shrimp juice (*saeu chŏt*) when it boils.

Pine Nut Porridge *Chat chuk,* 잣죽

1 cup rice, soaked for 1 hour
1 cup pine nuts
2 cups water

1. Grind soaked rice and pine nuts with 1 cup water in a blender. Strain into a pot for cooking. Add 1 cup water to what is left in the strainer and grind well so that there won't be much left when strained again. Strain.

2. Boil the strained liquid, stirring often. At the beginning, you might think it will be too thick, but don't add any water. It will become just right when cooked. Serve without salting so that diners can salt to their taste.

Regardless of how much *chuk* you make, just remember you need to use the same amount of pine nuts as rice and twice as much water and no more.

Sweet Bean Porridge *P'at chuk,* 팥죽

1 cup sweet beans (p'at)
½ cup soaked rice
1 cup glutinous rice powder (if you want to add rice dumplings)
1 tablespoon salt
water

1. Parboil sweet beans in 3 or 4 cups water on high flame and drain. (I do so because I've heard the skins of sweet beans contain some kind of toxic element.)

2. Add 10 cups water and boil until beans are cooked soft to the touch. Put the beans in a strainer and save the liquid. Add 1 tablespoon salt to the beans. Mash the beans in the strainer, adding cold water until you get 9 cups of liquid altogether; discard skins. Let the liquid stand so that the bean sediment will settle.

3. Pour the liquid, without the sediment, over soaked rice and boil. When the rice is cooked, add the sediment by the spoonful and boil, stirring often. The *chuk* is done when it has thickened.

4. If you want to add glutinous rice dumplings, knead glutinous rice powder with 2 or 3 tablespoons boiling water and a pinch of salt. Shape into balls ½ inch round and add to the *chuk* when it is almost done. Remove from the heat when the dumplings surface.

Makes 6 servings.

Note

If you want dumplings in your *chuk* but do not want to go to the trouble of making them, you can use store-bought *injŏlmi* cakes made of glutinous rice. Cut the *injŏlmi* into ½ inch cubes and add them when the *chuk* is almost done.

Some people add sugar to their *p'at chuk*.

P'at chuk is one of the most popular porridges today but it was a must on the winter solstice in the old days because of the folk belief that sweet beans expel evil spirits. By the same token, some people still make *p'at chuk* or *p'at ttŏk* rice cake when they move into a new house.

Mung Bean Porridge *Noktu chuk,* 녹두죽

1 cup whole, unpeeled mung beans
⅔ cup soaked rice
1 tablespoon salt
water

1. Boil mung beans in 10 cups water until beans are cooked soft to the touch, as for *p'at chuk*.

2. Mash the beans with your hands, add 1 tablespoon salt and strain, adding water until you have 8 cups of the sediment and the liquid; discard any skins remaining in the strainer.

3. Boil soaked rice with the bean liquid. It is easier to boil rice with the thin liquid part and add spoonfuls of sediment when the rice is cooked, stirring all the while. Some say that it tastes better if you boil rice with the sediment and all from the beginning, but that means a lot of hard stirring. I haven't tried both ways at the same time and compared the taste but, believe me, if there is any difference, it is not worth an aching arm.

They say *noktu chuk* lowers one's cholesterol considerably if it is eaten for a month.

Pumpkin Porridge
Hobak pŏmbŏk, 호박범벅

7 cups peeled and sliced pumpkin
½ cup sweet beans (**p'at**)
½ cup kidney beans (**kangnang k'ong**)
1 cup glutinous rice powder
1½ teaspoons salt
4 tablespoons sugar

1. Halve a pumpkin, remove the seeds. Cut the pumpkin into 1-inch-wide slices, slice off the skin and cut into 1-inch-square pieces.

2. Add 2 cups water to 7 cups pumpkin and boil on high heat for about 15 minutes, then lower the heat and simmer for 20 minutes until the pumpkin is tender.

3. Boil sweet beans in water till tender (four times as much water as beans).

4. Boil kidney beans the same as the sweet beans.

5. Mix ½ cup glutinous rice powder with 1 tablespoon of boiling water to make dough. Roll into balls about the size of a ginkgo nut. A half cup will make about 20 balls.

6. Blend another ½ cup glutinous rice powder with ½ cup water.

7. Mash the boiled pumpkin with a spatula, add boiled sweet beans and kidney beans and bring to a boil. Stir in rice powder and water mixture (6) and bring to a boil. Stir to the end to prevent scorching. Add salt, sugar and rice balls (5) and bring to a final boil before removing from heat.

Makes 6 servings.

Note
If the kidney beans are fresh, you don't need to boil them separately. They can be added directly to the pumpkin at the beginning.

You can make pumpkin porridge without beans. Just add the rice powder and water mixture when the mashed pumpkin is boiling. Glutinous sorghum balls can be used instead of rice balls. Prepare them the same way.

Make glutinous rice dough with water in which sweet beans were boiled. The balls will be tinted a pretty color.

Pickled Food *Chang-atchi*, 장아찌

Chang-atchi, or pickled vegetables, go very well with *chuk*. When one has no appetite, a small amount of one or two kinds of pickled vegetables works wonders to whet the taste buds. In the old days before refrigerators, *chang-atchi* were made very salty to preserve them, but nowadays they can be made far less salty if kept in the refrigerator.

Only 20 years ago, I never dreamed of pickling vegetables out of season because they were terribly expensive, if available at all. When we finished making *kimjang kimch'i* for winter, we would slice and dry the leftover radishes and cabbage roots for pickling. We also soaked perilla leaves in salt water for days to eliminate the bitter taste, dried and seasoned them. These days all kinds of vegetables are available in all seasons, so you can make any kind of *chang-atchi* whenever you want to have it. I still find it quite refreshing to mix cold, leftover rice in water and eat it with no other side dish but a little bit of *chang-atchi*.

White Korean Radish Pickle
Much'ae yŏt chang-atchi, 무채엿장아찌

4 cups white Korean radish, cut to finger size
1 cup soy sauce
3 tablespoons sugar
1 tablespoon sliced green onion
2 teaspoons garlic strips
2 teaspoons ginger strips
1 teaspoon red pepper powder

1. Pour soy sauce over radish and let stand overnight.

2. The next day, squeeze the soy sauce out of the radish strips and put them in a container.

3. Add sugar to the sauce and simmer until it is reduced down to about 1 cup. Cool and pour over the radish.

4. After 2 or 3 days, squeeze the radish again and bring the sauce to a boil and let cool. To the squeezed radish, add strips of green onions, ginger and garlic and fine red pepper powder and mix well. Place the radish back into the container and pour in the cooled sauce.

5. Serve in small portions, sprinkled with sesame salt and a drop of sesame oil.

Note

The reason I boil the soy sauce many times is to prevent the growth of fungus. If the pickles are to be kept in the refrigerator, three times should be enough.

Radish *chang-atchi* is usually made with dried radish strips, but this way eliminates the lengthy process of drying and you get the same result. It is also more convenient when you want to make just a small amount.

Because regular Korean soy sauce (*chin kanjang*) is not salty enough, I mix it with soup soy sauce (*kuk kanjang*), 1 part *kuk kanjang* to 3 parts *chin kanjang*, but the Japanese soy sauce available in American stores is salty enough.

Cucumber Pickle
Oi suk chang-atchi, 오이숙장아찌

pickle-size cucumbers or short, slender cucumbers
soy sauce
sugar
vinegar

1. Scrub cucumbers, rub them with salt, and rinse once. Layer them in a bottle or plastic container.

2. To determine how much soy sauce is needed, barely cover the cucumbers with water, pour it off and measure it. Pour that amount of soy sauce in a pan and add $\frac{1}{3}$ cup sugar and $\frac{1}{3}$ cup vinegar for every cup of soy sauce. Bring the mixture to a boil and pour over the cucumbers while it is still boiling so that the cucumbers will be crisp. Place wooden chopsticks or a bamboo net over the cucumbers and weigh them down with a heavy stone. Let stand overnight.

3. The next day, remove the cucumbers and reserve the liquid. Put the cucumbers back in the container, this time placing those that were on top on the bottom so that all of the cucumbers become evenly salted. Bring the liquid to a boil, cool completely and pour over the cucumbers. Repeat after 2 or 3 days.

4. To serve, cut pickled cucumbers into bite size pieces and sprinkle with sesame seeds, or mix with sesame oil, red pepper powder and chopped green onion.

Note
When you have only large cucumbers, you can pickle them after cutting them into bite size pieces from the beginning.

Pickled Green Pepper
Koch'u chang-atchi, 고추장아찌

crisp green peppers
sugar
vinegar
soy sauce

1. Snip the stems of green peppers about $\frac{1}{2}$ inch from the top. Snip off the tips so that the sauce can soak into the peppers. Place them layer upon layer in a container.

2. Boil soy sauce, sugar and vinegar at the rate of 3:1:1, the same as when making cucumber pickles (previous page). Pour the sauce over the green peppers after it has cooled. Unlike cucumbers, peppers will cook if boiling sauce is poured over them. Let stand 2 days. Pour out the sauce, boil, cool and pour back over the peppers. Repeat after 3 or 4 days.

Note
You can pickle green peppers with cucumbers, putting them at the bottom of the container under the cucumbers. In fact, it enhances the cucumber pickle because green peppers add a spicy, provocative flavor.

Koreans are great *namul* eaters. They eat almost all kinds of vegetables, herbs, and young sprouts of trees prepared in all kinds of manner: boiled, steamed, sautéed, fresh or tossed with *yangnyŏmjang* sauce. Some vegetables are dried in season and soaked and boiled for cooking when they are out of season. They provide much needed vitamins and minerals during winter.

Namul made of dried vegetables are a must for a First Full Moon dinner when one is supposed to eat at least 5 to 9 kinds of vegetables in addition to *ogok pap*, glutinous rice cooked with 5 kinds of beans and grains. (Note that everything comes in odd numbers, because odd numbers are considered lucky.) According to a folk belief, the smell of boiling dried vegetables, especially radish leaves, on the First Full Moon day prevents evil spirits from entering the house.

To cook dried vegetables, soak in lukewarm water and let stand until they become soft. Boil once and cool. When they are soft to the touch, pour out the water and soak in fresh water again to eliminate the bitter taste. Squeeze the water out, cut into easy-to-eat pieces and sauté.

4 cups **kosari** *or* **kobi** *(shoots slightly thicker than* **kosari***), soaked and boiled in water*
½ cup beef broth
4 green onions, cut into 2-inch pieces, sliced lengthwise

A. *2 tablespoons soy sauce*
   1 teaspoon chopped garlic
   2 tablespoons cooking oil
   dash black pepper

B. *1 tablespoon sesame oil*
   1 tablespoon sesame salt
   1 teaspoon red pepper powder
   ¼ teaspoon black pepper

1. Clean *kosari* or *kobi*, remove the hard, lower part of the stems and cut into 2-inch pieces. Add (A) seasonings and mix well using your hands in a kneading fashion.

2. Sauté in a pan for 5 minutes on medium heat. Add beef broth. Cover and simmer, turning now and then until liquid is gone. Turn the heat off, add sliced green onion and cover. When the green onion strips become soft, mix with (B) seasonings.

Note

You might want to add minced beef seasoned with the *pulgogi* seasoning minus sugar when you sauté *kosari*.

The broth should taste rather bland when *kosari* is being sautéed. If it tastes just right, the *kosari* will turn out salty. Try with my measurements the first time and then increase or decrease the seasoning to your taste. Soy sauce varies slightly in saltiness according to brand. I am just trying to give you the basics for making *namul*.

You can make *namul* the same way with dried zucchini slices, sweet potato sprouts, and *ch'wi namul* (young leaves of a kind of aster).

4 cups bellflower roots (**toraji**)
1 tablespoon cooking oil
1 tablespoon soy sauce
1 tablespoon soup soy sauce
$\frac{1}{2}$ cup broth
2 tablespoons chopped green onions
1 teaspoon chopped garlic
$\frac{1}{4}$ teaspoon black pepper
1 tablespoon sesame salt
1 teaspoon red pepper strips (**shilgoch'u**)
1 tablespoon sesame oil

1. If dried, soak the *toraji* roots in lukewarm water until soft and shred to chopstick thinness to make 4 cups. If fresh, knead with coarse salt and soak in water to eliminate bitter taste. Some *toraji* roots are so bitter that you will have to soak 2 or 3 days.

2. Heat oil. Add garlic and stir-fry. Add soy sauce and soup soy sauce. When the mixture boils, add *toraji* and simmer until slightly soft, adding broth a little at a time to prevent scorching. Add sliced green onions and mix. Sprinkle with black pepper, sesame salt, red pepper strips and sesame oil.

Note

Toraji is often sautéed with salt instead of soy sauce. Some people like it better because it retains its white color, but I am used to doing it with soy sauce and like the taste better.

Toraji is sometimes parboiled prior to sautéing. I don't parboil it, however, because that makes it too soft when simmered. If you like your *namul* soft, parboil it first.

Toraji namul tastes even more delicious if you first fry minced beef, seasoned with *pulgogi* seasoning (but with very little sugar), and then add *toraji* and sauté.

Scalded Spinach
Shigŭmch'i namul, 시금치나물

1 pound spinach
8 cups water with 1 tablespoon table salt
2 tablespoons red pepper paste
1 tablespoon vinegar
1 tablespoon honey
1 tablespoon chopped green onion
1 tablespoon sesame salt

1. Scald spinach in salted water. Rinse in cold water and drain. (When you scald spinach, turn the heat off as soon as you put the spinach in the boiling water and turn over once. If you keep the heat on until the water comes to a boil again, the spinach will become too soft and lose its freshness.)

2. Mix red pepper paste, vinegar and honey. Add salt if you find the mixture too bland or sweet. Pour the mixture on the drained spinach and mix well. Add chopped green onion and sesame salt and mix one more time.

Variation
If you don't have red pepper paste, mix the spinach with 1 teaspoon soy sauce, 1 teaspoon salt ($\frac{1}{2}$ teaspoon table salt), 1 teaspoon sugar, 2 teaspoons vinegar, 1 teaspoon red pepper powder, 2 teaspoons chopped green onion, and 1 tablespoon sesame salt.

Note
Bellflower roots, garland chrysanthemums and thread green onions are also very good when scalded and mixed with vinegar, red pepper paste and honey in the same combination as the scalded spinach.

Young Shoots of Bracken
Scalded Spinach   Bellflower Roots
Kosari namul
Shigŭmchi namul   *Toraji namul*

117

Sautéed Cucumber
Oi paetturi, 오이뱃두리

8 cups of sliced cucumber
1 tablespoon table salt
4 ounces ($\frac{1}{2}$ cup) minced beef
pinch red pepper threads
2 teaspoons sesame oil
1 tablespoon sesame salt

A. $\frac{1}{2}$ tablespoon soy sauce
   $\frac{1}{2}$ tablespoon sugar
   1 teaspoon chopped green onion
   1 teaspoon chopped garlic
   1 teaspoon sesame salt
   1 teaspoon sesame oil
   1 teaspoon rice wine
   dash black pepper

1. Cut cucumbers into disks about $\frac{1}{8}$-inch thick. Mix with salt and let stand.

2. Season minced beef with (A) ingredients. Knead well to mix.

3. Put salted cucumber in a cloth sack or wrap in a piece of cloth and squeeze hard until the cucumber slices are crisp. If they are not squeezed enough, they become limp when sautéed; if they are squeezed too much, they will lose the fresh cucumber flavor.

4. Stir-fry seasoned meat; when the meat is half done, add the cucumber. When the cucumber becomes bright green, add red pepper strips and sesame oil. Stir once before removing from the heat. You might want to sprinkle the cooked cucumber with sesame salt.

Note
If you find the cucumber too salty, soak them in water before squeezing. If too bland, add more salt and wait. If you squeeze the cucumber pieces before they are salty enough, they will smell like crushed vegetables. Don't worry if they taste too salty or too bland after they are squeezed because you can adjust the taste with the seasoning of the minced beef.

White Korean Radish Strips
Mu saengch'ae, 무생채

$\frac{1}{2}$ *medium size white Korean radish*
   (2 cups when sliced into strips)
1 teaspoon table salt
2 teaspoons red pepper powder
1 tablespoon chopped green onion
1 tablespoon sesame salt

A. 1 tablespoon vinegar
   2 tablespoons sugar
   $\frac{1}{2}$ *teaspoon ginger juice*

1. Cut white Korean radish into matchstick strips. To make strips, first cut the whole radish into chunks about 2 inches thick, halve them lengthwise, slice each half lengthwise into $\frac{1}{8}$-inch-thick sheets and slice them lengthwise again to the same thickness. (Or why not forget it all and use a shredder or a food processor!) Sprinkle with salt and let stand for about 15minutes. Squeeze lightly.

2. Add red pepper powder and mix well to tint radish evenly.

3. In a bowl, mix (A) ingredients thoroughly. Pour the mixture over the radish strips. Add chopped green onions and sesame salt and mix.

Variation
Cut radish into 2-inch-thick chunks, slice lengthwise into the thinnest sheets you can make. Cut cucumber and carrot into strips. Make 1 generous cup each. Soak all three in a mixture of 1 tablespoon vinegar, $\frac{1}{2}$ teaspoon salt, 1 tablespoon sugar, 1 teaspoon ginger juice and 1 tablespoon water. Let stand for about 15 minutes. Place a few carrot and cucumber strips on radish sheet and roll. Secure each roll by piercing through with a toothpick. Pour the liquid in which they were soaked over the rolls and serve.

This recipe is very refreshing when served together with fried food.

Dried Radish Leaves
Shiraegi namul, 시래기나물

4 cups boiled radish leaves
1 cup broth

A. *1 tablespoon soybean paste* (**toenjang**)
   1 tablespoon anchovy powder
   1 tablespoon chopped garlic
   2 tablespoons cooking oil
   2 or 3 green peppers, seeded and sliced

B. *½ cup sliced green onions*
   1 tablespoon sesame salt
   1 tablespoon sesame oil
   1 teaspoon red pepper powder

1. Cut radish leaves in strips about 2 inches long. Add (A) ingredients, mix with your hands in a kneading fashion, and sauté. Add soup stock and simmer over medium to low heat.

2. When liquid is almost gone, mix with (B) ingredients. Remove from heat.

Note
When you have radish leaves left from making *kkaktugi* (radish *kimch'i*), scald them in salt water and then soak in cold water for a day to eliminate the odor. Pack in plastic bags and freeze.

In Korea we dry them during the winter *kimch'i* season when they come in great quantities. Then, when we want to cook *shiraegi*, the dried radish leaves, we boil them to make them soft. Though I can't say that the smell of boiling *shiraegi* is the best smell in the world, it tastes very good when cooked. Besides, *shiraegi* is loaded with vitamins and calcium.

Sautéed Zucchini *Hobak namul,* 호박나물

2 cups zucchini peels, cut into strips
¼ cup green pepper, cut into strips
½ teaspoon pickled shrimp (**saeu chŏt**)
1 tablespoon green onions
½ teaspoon table salt
1 tablespoon chopped garlic
1 teaspoon red pepper powder
1 tablespoon sesame salt
2 teaspoons sesame oil

1. Cut zucchini across into 2-inch-long chunks. Use only the firm outer part: pare carefully with about ⅛-inch-thick flesh of zucchini attached to the peel. Slice the peel into thin strips. Sprinkle with salt.

2. Cut green pepper lengthwise, remove seeds and cut to the same size as the zucchini strips.

3. Squeeze the salted zucchini. (It will become about ½ cup). Heat a little oil in a pan, add chopped garlic, and stir-fry squeezed zucchini quickly (1or 2 minutes) over strong heat. If you find zucchini too bland, add ½ teaspoon of pickled shrimp sauce (*saeu chŏt*). Add slices of green onion, sesame salt and red pepper powder.

Note
Zucchini will have a better flavor if stir-fried in perilla oil.

The unused inner part of the zucchini can be made into a nice dish too. Halve the chunks lengthwise and cut across into half-moon shapes (2 average-size zucchinis will make about 3 cups). Pour oil in a heated pan and sauté, adding 1½ tablespoons pickled shrimp, 1 teaspoon chopped garlic and a little red pepper powder, until the zucchini becomes juicy. Turn off the heat, add chopped green onion and sesame salt.

Of course this recipe can be also made with unpeeled zucchinis.

1

2

3

Mixed Vegetables *Chapch'ae,* 잡채

You don't have to use all of the following mushrooms and vegetables. Three or four kinds of contrasting color, added to the beef and mung bean noodles, will do nicely.

$\frac{1}{2}$ *pound lean beef*
2 cups (soaked) mung bean or potato noodles
  (**tangmyŏn**)
4 dried oak mushrooms (**p'yogo**)
5 fresh oyster mushrooms (**nŭt'ari**)
2 tablespoons dried Jew's ear mushrooms (**mogi**)
1 cup onion, sliced
1 cup carrot, cut in strips
4 cups bellflower roots
2 cups cucumber, sliced
$\frac{1}{2}$ *Korean pear*

A. 3 tablespoons soy sauce
   2 tablespoons sugar
   1 tablespoon honey (or $\frac{1}{2}$ tablespoon more sugar)

2 tablespoons pear juice (or 1 tablespoon rice wine)
1 tablespoon sesame oil
1 tablespoon sesame salt
$\frac{1}{2}$ *teaspoon black pepper*
2 tablespoons chopped green onion
1 teaspoon ginger juice
1 teaspoon chopped garlic

cooking oil, soy sauce, salt, black pepper, sugar, sesame oil

1. Make *yangnyŏmjang* sauce by mixing (A) ingredients.

2. Cut beef into thin strips about 2 inches long.

3. Add 4 tablespoons of the sauce to the sliced beef and knead to mix flavors. Stir-fry quickly in a heated pan. Remove from the pan as soon as the color of the meat changes. The meat will become tasteless if fried until the meat juice is all gone.

4. Soak noodles in lukewarm water and, when they lose their stiffness, cut into 3-inch-long pieces. Stir-fry in 5 tablespoons *yangnyŏmjang* sauce, 1 tablespoon oil and $\frac{1}{4}$ cup water.

5. Soak *p'yogo* mushrooms and *mogi* mushrooms in warm water. When *p'yogo* become soft, remove stems and slice into thin strips. Squeeze lightly. About $\frac{1}{4}$ cup will do. Mix with $\frac{1}{2}$ tablespoon each of soy sauce, sugar and sesame oil and a dash of pepper and stir-fry on medium heat. Two

tablespoons of dry *mogi* will become about $\frac{1}{3}$ cup when soaked for 30 minutes. Stir-fry *mogi*, adding $\frac{1}{2}$ teaspoon of salt and a dash of pepper.

6. Scald *nŭt'ari* mushrooms in salt water, rinse in cold water and shred. Make $\frac{1}{3}$ cup when squeezed lightly. Season with $\frac{1}{4}$ teaspoon salt, 1 teaspoon sesame oil and a dash of pepper. Stir-fry in a heated pan.

7. Cut onion in half and slice lengthwise into thin strips. Make 1 cup. Pour 1 teaspoon of oil in a pan and fry onion strips with 1 teaspoon of salt ($\frac{1}{2}$ teaspoon table salt). They will burn easily if the heat is too high. Stir-fry on medium to low heat and keep adding spoonfuls of water if they start to burn.

8. Cut cucumber into 5-inch-long chunks and peel. (Use only the skins.) Slice cucumber skin into thin strips. Make 2 cups. Salt the strips with 1 teaspoon table salt. When they have wilted, squeeze tightly in cloth and, in a pan greased with 1 teaspoon of oil, stir-fry quickly on high heat. Spread on a large dish to cool.

9. Cut carrot into 5-inch-long chunks and slice into thin strips. Make 1 cup. Stir-fry in a greased pan on medium heat, adding a little water now and then. Season with $\frac{1}{2}$ teaspoon table salt. Spread on a large dish to cool.

10. Cut bellflower roots into 2-inch lengths. Scald in boiling salt water, rinse and slice into thin strips. Pour oil in a pan and when the oil is heated, stir-fry bellflower roots with $\frac{1}{2}$ teaspoon chopped garlic and 1 teaspoon salt. Add 1 tablespoon chopped green onion, 1 tablespoon sesame salt and a dash of pepper when cooked.

11. When all ingredients are ready, put the noodles in a large mixing bowl, add 1 tablespoon of *yangnyŏmjang* sauce and fried beef, and then mix in the vegetables.

Chapch'ae can be very refreshing if strips of pear are added at this point. If you want to make it even more colorful, you can add egg strips, fine strips of stone mushroom *(sŏgi)*, and/or pine nut powder

½ pound lean beef or pork
¼ cup carrots, sliced in strips
¼ cup onions, sliced in strips
½ cup zucchini, sliced in strips
¼ cup bell pepper, sliced in strips
1 cup Chinese chives, cut in 2- to 3-inch lengths
*¼ cup **p'yogo** mushrooms, soaked*
2 cups mung bean or potato noodles, soaked
2 teaspoons chopped garlic
¼ cup green onion, cut lengthwise into 2-inch-long pieces
3 or 4 tablespoons cooking oil
3 tablespoons soy sauce
1 teaspoon sesame oil

1. Slice beef into strips about 2 inches long. Slice vegetables likewise.

2. Soak mushrooms in warm water until soft. Slice and squeeze lightly. (Save the water in which mushrooms were soaked. It is good to add to soup or *tchigae*. When you are in a hurry, add a spoonful of sugar to the water and the mushrooms will become tender much faster.)

3. Soak noodles in warm water until soft. Cut into about 3-inch-long pieces.

4. Heat oil in a pre-heated wok. Add chopped garlic and green onion. The oil will become permeated with their fragrance. Add the meat and stir-fry. When the meat is almost done, add mushrooms.

Add the remaining vegetables except the chives, the hardest first and the softest last. When the vegetables are done, add the drained noodles. If there is not much liquid in the wok, add beef broth so that the noodles will cook. Season with soy sauce after the noodles are done. About 2 tablespoons of soy sauce will be enough for 3 cups of *chapch'ae* (when measured by the eye).

5. Add Chinese chives, stir once. Add sesame oil before serving.

This recipe takes only 5 to 10 minutes to cook if you have the ingredients prepared and ready in the refrigerator. I recommend this recipe when you don't have much time.

Note

Add the carrot, onion, zucchini and bell pepper in that order and any other vegetables that you have. *Chapch'ae* means "various vegetables" and it is just that. You can throw in some cauliflower and broccoli if you want, only do so when you start to fry the meat because they are rather hard.

On the other hand, you don't have to have all the various vegetables. Pork, Chinese chives and potato noodles are enough to make pork *chapch'ae*. Or you can make green pepper *chapch'ae* with just meat and slices of green pepper. Just use a little imagination, and you can create *chapch'ae* with almost anything.

Acorn Jelly *Tot'ori muk,* 도토리묵

1 pack acorn jelly
10 perilla leaves
$\frac{1}{2}$ *cucumber*
1 tablespoon sesame oil
$\frac{1}{2}$ *teaspoon salt*

yangnyŏmjang *sauce*
   3 tablespoons soy sauce
   3 tablespoons chopped green onion
   $\frac{1}{2}$ *teaspoon chopped garlic*
   $\frac{1}{2}$ *teaspoon vinegar*
   $\frac{1}{2}$ *teaspoon sugar*
   2 teaspoons red pepper powder
   2 teaspoons sesame salt

1. Cut acorn jelly (*tot'ori muk*) into $2 \times 1 \times \frac{1}{2}$ inch pieces. Arrange the pieces on a plate, brush with sesame oil and sprinkle with salt.

2. Cut cucumber into thin strips and sprinkle over the jelly.

3. Make *yangnyŏmjang* and pour it over the jelly and cucumber. Serve.

Note

You may want to spread perilla leaves on the plate before you put the pieces of acorn jelly on it, or cut them into strips and place them over the jelly before you add the *yangnyŏmjang*.

I add a little vinegar to the *yangnyŏmjang* because it helps remove the smell of the soy sauce. I also find it tastes better when I use a little sugar, but it all depends on individual taste. I don't put garlic in the *yangnyŏmjang* for acorn jelly, but all my friends insist garlic should go in.

How to make *tot'ori muk*

Although *muk* is available in stores, I always make it at home because store-bought *muk* is usually not made with just acorn powder but with a mixture of other powders. Some people say it doesn't matter because *muk* itself is almost tasteless, that what is important is the *yangnyŏmjang*. But making your own *muk* can be very satisfying. You will see that *muk* made with pure acorn powder is bouncier than store-bought *muk*.

1 cup acorn powder
6 cups water
$\frac{1}{2}$ *teaspoon salt*

1. Mix acorn powder with water. Blend well and let stand for awhile. In fact, if you place the mixture in the refrigerator for a couple of days, the final product will be bouncy.

2. Sieve into a pan and boil. Stir constantly, being careful to scrape the bottom of the pan to prevent burning. When it begins to boil, reduce heat to

low. Cover and simmer over very low heat, lifting the cover only to stir once every 2 minutes. Let simmer at least 25 minutes. The longer it simmers, the bouncier it will be. I sometimes let it simmer as long as 40 minutes. When it is almost done, add 2 teaspoons of salt and stir.

3. Rinse a square pan in cold water and pour the boiled acorn liquid into it to cool. Do not put it in the refrigerator because the *muk* will stiffen and taste dull. If you want to cool it quickly, put the pan in cold water and change the water frequently.

Mung Bean Jelly *Ch'ŏngp'o muk,* 청포묵

1 pack mung bean jelly (**ch'ŏngp'o muk**)
4 ounces beef ($\frac{1}{2}$ *cup when sliced*)
$\frac{1}{2}$ *cup* **minari**, *scalded*
1 cup mung bean sprouts
1 cup cucumber skin, sliced
salt, soy sauce, sugar, vinegar, sesame oil, sesame salt, pepper, red pepper threads, chopped green onion, chopped garlic

1. Cut mung bean jelly (*ch'ŏngp'o muk*) into chopstick-thin sticks about 2 inches long. Make 2 cups. Season with 2 teaspoons sesame oil and a pinch of salt.

2. Remove the heads and hairy ends of the mung bean sprouts. Scald the sprouts; 1 cup of fresh sprouts will become $\frac{1}{2}$ cup when scalded. Marinate in a mixture of 1 teaspoon salt, 1 tablespoon sugar, 1 teaspoon vinegar and 2 teaspoons water.

3. Scald tender stalks of *minari* in salt water, rinse in cold water and squeeze. Cut into 2-inch-long pieces. Season with $\frac{1}{2}$ teaspoon salt.

4. Cut the cucumbers across into 2-inch-long chunks and carefully peel off the skin and the firm outer part of the flesh. (Do not use the seedy inside.) Slice the skin into thin strips. Salt with $\frac{1}{2}$ teaspoon salt and, after awhile, squeeze tightly. Season with 1 teaspoon sugar and 1 teaspoon vinegar.

5. Cut lean beef into thin strips. Season with 2 teaspoons soy sauce, $1\frac{1}{2}$ teaspoons sugar, 1 teaspoon sesame oil, 1 teaspoon sesame salt, 1 teaspoon chopped green onion, and $\frac{1}{2}$ teaspoon chopped garlic. Stir-fry.

6. When the fried beef has cooled, mix with mung bean sprouts, *minari* and cucumber; and then mix lightly with slivers of *muk*. Sprinkle with a pinch of red pepper threads.

You might like it better if the *muk* strips are sprinkled with sea laver, roasted and crushed into small pieces.

How to make *ch'ŏngp'o muk*

1 cup **muk** *powder*
7 cups water
1 teaspoon salt

You will need 7 cups of water for 1 cup of powder. Mix 1 cup of powder in 4 cups of water. Blend well and sieve. Boil 3 cups of water in a pan. When the water begins to boil, stir in the sieved liquid. When it begins to bubble, cover and simmer over low heat for about 20 minutes. Stir all the way to the bottom every 2 or 3 minutes, keeping it covered in between. Add 1 teaspoon of salt before removing from the heat. Pour the hot mixture into a square, wet vessel, cover with plastic wrap and allow to cool.

Do not use an oily pan or an oily spatula because *muk* does not thicken well when it comes in contact with oil.

When you find leftover *muk* has hardened, do not throw it away; it will soften and become as good as new if scalded in hot water.

Mung bean jelly works wonders for the side effects of herbal medicine; likewise, it will cancel out any good effects. The same goes for *pindaettŏk* (mung bean pancake).

Fresh Vegetables with Sauce
Kŏtchŏri, 겉절이

Romaine, iceberg, or Korean lettuce, garland chrysanthemum (**ssukkat**), *alfalfa sprouts, radish sprouts, thread green onions* (**shilp'a**), *perilla leaves* (**kkaennip**), *button mushrooms, dandelions, or any other vegetables that can make fresh salad*

A. *2 tablespoons soy sauce*
    2 tablespoons vinegar
    2 tablespoons sugar
    2 tablespoons anchovy sauce (**myŏlch'i chŏt**)
    1 tablespoon red pepper powder
    1 tablespoon sesame salt

1. Make sauce with (A) ingredients.

2. Mix sauce with any combination of fresh vegetables available. The sauce will be enough for 12 cups of cut vegetables.

This sauce is not rich in oil like American salad dressings. Remember to toss the salad right before serving. Do not add oil because it does not go well with this sauce.

Note
Japanese soybean paste *(toenjang)* dressing is also worth a try.

4 tablespoons Japanese bean paste
2 tablespoons sugar
2 tablespoons cooking oil
3 tablespoons rice vinegar
1 tablespoon sesame oil
$\frac{1}{2}$ teaspoon salt
$\frac{1}{2}$ teaspoon black pepper

Blend ingredients in a blender and sprinkle with sesame salt when mixing with vegetables.

Stir-fried Potatoes
Kamja namul, 감자나물

2 large potatoes
5 green peppers
½ onion
1 tablespoon cooking oil or perilla oil (**tǔl kirǔm**)
1 teaspoon chopped garlic
1 tablespoon chopped green onion
1 tablespoon sesame salt
dash black pepper
½ cup water

1. Peel potatoes and slice into strips. Two fist sized potatoes will make a little over 2 cups strips. Mix 2 tablespoons coarse salt in 2 cups cold water and soak potato strips in it for 15 minutes.

2. Open green peppers, shake out the seeds and cut into thin strips. Cut onion into strips.

3. When potato strips have softened, rinse in cold water and drain.

4. Pour cooking oil or perilla oil into a heated pan and add chopped garlic. Stir-fry potato and onion, adding water 3 or 4 times for a total of ½ cup. When the potato is cooked, add green pepper strips. Remove from heat when the pepper strips have turned bright green; add chopped green onion, black pepper and sesame salt.

Note
Potatoes become softer and taste better if squeezed after being soaked in salt water, but they will break while being squeezed. The reason for soaking them in salt water is to prevent them from sticking to the pan during cooking. Potatoes will cook well if water is added little by little. They will break if covered while cooking.

1 ½ cups cucumbers, sliced (Select thin cucumbers)
1 teaspoon salt
1 tablespoon vinegar
5 teaspoons sugar
1 tablespoon red pepper powder
1 tablespoon chopped green onion
1 tablespoon sesame salt

1. Wash cucumbers well, scrubbing with salt. Halve them lengthwise and cut diagonally into $\frac{1}{16}$-inch thick pieces.

2. Make sauce by mixing salt, vinegar, and sugar. Mix until sugar dissolves.

3. Mix cucumber slices thoroughly with the sauce. Add red pepper powder, chopped green onion and sesame salt, and mix again.

Note

It is better not to add garlic when cucumber is mixed fresh such as in this recipe.

Thin cucumbers are preferable because they have fewer seeds. Some cucumbers are bitter. Taste a piece from the stem end before you slice the whole cucumber.

This recipe is useful when you don't have *kimch'i.*

Chestnut Salad
Pam much'im, 밤무침

1 cup chestnuts, cut into slivers
$\frac{3}{4}$ cup cucumber, sliced
$\frac{1}{4}$ cup onion, sliced

Sauce
   1 teaspoon salt
   3 tablespoons vinegar
   5 tablespoons sugar
   2 teaspoons red pepper powder
   2 teaspoons sesame salt
   1 tablespoon chopped green onion

1. Peel chestnuts, wash and soak in water to prevent discoloring. Drain and cut into $\frac{1}{16}$-inch-thick slivers.

2. Cut the outer part of the cucumbers about the same size as the chestnut slivers. (Do not use the seedy inside.)

3. Cut onion the same size as the chestnut slivers.

4. Make sauce by mixing the sauce ingredients.

5. Add the chestnuts, cucumbers and onion to the sauce in that order.

Note

Small wild onions (*tallae*) and/or roast beef, cut the size of the chestnut slivers, are a good addition.

This recipe is better when garlic is not added.

Kimch'i 김치

Korea is the country of *kimch'i*. Everyone thinks of *kimch'i* when it comes to Korean cooking. It is said that one can tell a great deal about a housewife from the taste of her *kimch'i* and sauces. When you are invited to someone's house, you can indeed tell if your hostess is a good cook or not by tasting her *kimch'i*.

It is said that children avoid *kimch'i* these days. I think it is because their mothers make it without caring how it tastes or buy it, not even bothering to make it themselves.

The first thing in making good *kimch'i* is to use good red pepper powder. Giving it just the right degree of saltiness is also very important. I suggest you use only a minimum amount of garlic and ginger. If you work with Westerners, *kimch'i* with a lot of garlic can get you into an embarrassing situation because your breath will smell even when you keep your mouth closed, to say nothing of when you speak. Why put in a lot of garlic when you can make everyone happy with a little less garlic, which actually makes little difference in the taste? Some Koreans insist that Western cheeses can be even more smelly than *kimch'i*, but they smell only when they are being eaten and the odor does not linger the whole day.

Dr. Okgill Kim, the late president of Ewha University, used to have her *kimch'i* made without green onions or garlic, just salt and red pepper powder, but it was very delicious. The point is to use the right amount of salt. Don't use table salt if you can help it because it tends to make *kimch'i* a little bitter. Roasted salt is the most healthful but if not available, plain white salt will do. (Also remember table salt is twice as salty as the roasted or plain salt.) Mind not to make it so red that it makes people's eyes tear. And don't use too much fish sauce because the *kimch'i* won't stay fresh but become rather rancid. Fresh or frozen shrimps are better than fish sauce.

When you make *kimch'i*, wait a day or two before you put it in the refrigerator to give it a chance to start ripening. *Kimch'i* will get "frost-bitten" and become unpalatable if refrigerated before it starts to ferment. This is another reason why young people dislike *kimch'i*. Grown-ups tend to put it in the refrigerator when it is still fresh because they cannot tolerate sour *kimch'i* whereas young people like it only when it is sour.

There are all kinds of *kimch'i* made with all kinds of vegetables, not just the commonly known Korean cabbage, radish and cucumber, but such improbable things as eggplant and pumpkin. I have included only the kinds that are simple to make. Start with easy ones and, with practice, you will soon be able to make more complicated ones. After all, the basic seasoning is the same for most *kimch'i*. I have been making *kimch'i* for over 30 years, yet I have not been able to make *kimch'i* taste exactly the same every time because I guess the taste of the cabbage and radish differ, the weather differs and the salting and rinsing differ every time.

Pre-Cut Cabbage *Kimch'i*
Paech'u mak kimch'i, 배추막김치

6 pounds or 3 medium-sized Korean cabbages
3 cups coarse salt
12 cups water
1 tablespoon chopped garlic
1 tablespoon chopped ginger
3 tablespoons green onion, cut to $\frac{1}{2}$ -inch lengths
1 cup red pepper powder
$\frac{3}{4}$ cup fish sauce (**myŏlch'i chŏt**)
1 cup fresh shrimp, finely chopped
3 tablespoons sugar

1. Cut cabbages lengthwise into two sections. Mix 2 cups of coarse salt in 12 cups water and soak cabbages in it for about 15 minutes. Sprinkle the remaining 1 cup coarse salt between the leaves at the stem end and let stand for 4 to 5 hours, bringing the ones in the bottom to the top from time to time so that the cabbages will be evenly salted. If cabbages are very large, you might need to wait longer than that for the firm part to wilt, maybe as long as 8 hours.

2. Crush or chop garlic and ginger. Cut green onions into about $1\frac{1}{2}$-inch lengths. Chop fresh shrimp finely.

3. When cabbages are limp, rinse thoroughly 3 or 4 times and drain. Cut into about 1- to $1\frac{1}{2}$-inch squares.

4. In a large bowl, mix the cabbage squares with red pepper powder to tint the cabbage. Then add fish sauce and the garlic, ginger, and shrimps and mix. Add green onion pieces and sugar. Mix again.

If the cabbage is too salty, do not add fish sauce. Taste the *kimch'i* the next day and if it is salty, add 2 or 3 cups soup stock. If too bland, salt the soup stock or add some soup soy sauce.

For a bright red *kimch'i*, soak red pepper powder in fish sauce and let stand for 1 hour before mixing with other ingredients.

Do not put in the refrigerator at first, but leave at room temperature until it begins to ferment.

Note

This is a simpler way to make *kimch'i*. The traditional way is to use salted cabbages cut lengthwise in half or quarters and not in small pieces, and rub in the spiced stuffing between the leaves as the one in the photograph, but I thought it was too complicated because you would have to cut radishes into thin strips for stuffing and then cut the *kimch'i* to bite size every time you serve it. If you were to make winter *kimch'i*, which we make in a great quantity at the beginning of winter when the cabbages are still cheap and store in pottery jars buried up to the neck in the backyard to last us through the winter and sometimes to the end of the spring, you must use the large pieces of cabbage. But short of that, pre-cut *kimch'i* is much more convenient to make and to serve.

Hot Radish *Kimch'i*   *Kkaktugi,* 깍두기

2 pounds Korean white radish, regular or small
1 tablespoon salt
4 tablespoons red pepper powder
3 tablespoons green onion, sliced
$\frac{1}{2}$ teaspoon chopped garlic
$\frac{1}{2}$ teaspoon crushed ginger
2 tablespoons fresh or frozen shrimp
4 tablespoons fish sauce (**myŏlch'i chŏt**)
1 tablespoon sugar

1. Cut radish into about $\frac{1}{2}$- to $\frac{3}{4}$-inch cubes; 2
   pounds will make about 8 cups. Sprinkle the
   cubes with salt and toss up and down to mix. Let
   stand about 20 minutes and drain. (Sometimes
   you will find radishes taste bitter. If you do, rinse
   them once at this stage to get rid of the bitter
   taste.) Rub in red pepper powder to thint the
   radish cubes.

2. Cut green onions to the length of the radish
   cubes, chop garlic and ginger. Chop fresh or
   frozen shrimp.

3. Add these ingredients to the radish cubes together
   with fish sauce and sugar. Mix well.

4. Leave the finished *kkaktugi* at room temperature.
   After a day, taste the juice to see if it has begun to
   ferment. If it has, store the *kkaktugi* in the
   refrigerator for 5 to 7 days for further fermentation
   before serving.

Note

Radish leaves are very good when mixed in the
kkaktugi. Cut them a little longer than the *kkaktugi*
cubes. They can also be used as is. In this case, mix
the leaves with 1 tablespoon of shrimp sauce and 1
tablespoon of red pepper powder. Place all of them
at the bottom of the container and put the *kkaktugi*
on them. By the time you finish the *kkaktugi*, the
leaves will have been nicely fermented.

If you want to use brown sugar instead of white
sugar, increase the amount slightly.

Onion slices make *kkaktugi* more delicious but they
also make it sour faster. When you add onions, use
a little less green onion.

Stuffed Cucumber *Kimch'i*
Oi sobagi, 오이소박이

10 medium size cucumbers (pickling cucumbers or long
   Japanese cucumbers; never use cucumbers that are
   fat and zucchini-like or English cucumbers)
2 cups Korean white radish, cut into strips
coarse salt
1 tablespoon table salt
1 tablespoon sugar
1 tablespoon red pepper powder
1 teaspoon chopped garlic
$\frac{1}{2}$ teaspoon chopped ginger
$\frac{1}{4}$ cup finely cut thread green onion

1. Wash cucumbers. Rub them with coarse salt and
   let stand for 10 to 15 minutes.

2. Cut radish into thin strips 1 inch long. To 2 cups
   of radish strips, add salt, sugar, red pepper
   powder, chopped garlic, chopped ginger and
   thread green onion. Mix well.

3. Rinse cucumbers and cut them into 2-inch-long
   chunks. Slit each chunk from one end down to
   about $\frac{2}{3}$ the whole length and repeat from the
   other end, this time at a right angle to the other
   cut so that the pieces will not break apart. Fill the
   cuts with the radish mixture.

4. Boil $\frac{1}{2}$ cup of water. Pour the boiling water into
   the empty bowl you used to mix the radish to get
   all the leftover seasoning and pour the water, still
   hot, over the stuffed cucumbers.

Note

You may want to add 2 tablespoons of finely grated
onion when you make the radish stuffing. Stuffing is
usually made with chives but I find radish stuffing
makes the cucumber *kimch'i* fresher. The reason I
use boiling hot water is because it makes the
cucumber crispy.

Young Radish *Kimch'i*
Yŏlmu kimch'i, 열무김치

3 bundles (3 pounds) young radish leaves (**yŏlmu**)
2 tablespoons red pepper powder
5 thin green onions
1 clove garlic
4 or 5 green peppers
ginger the size of garlic
$\frac{3}{4}$ cup roasted salt
$\frac{1}{4}$ cup sugar
$\frac{1}{4}$ cup flour
16 cups water

1. Boil 12 cups water with $\frac{1}{4}$ cup roasted salt and $\frac{1}{4}$ cup sugar. Blend flour with 1 cup water with a wire whisk or a spoon and add to the water when it boils to make a thin gruel. Sieve and let cool.

2. Cut *yŏlmu* into 2-inch-long pieces starting from the root end to make 16 cups. (Do not use the tough outer leaves at the other end; they can be scalded in salt water and made into soup.) Soak the *yŏlmu* pieces in a generous amount of water and wash well, rinsing several times. Sprinkle with $\frac{1}{2}$ cup roasted salt and let stand for 40 minutes.

3. After salting the *yŏlmu*, wash thin green onions and cut them the same size as the *yŏlmu*. Slice garlic into thin strips. Slice about the same amount of ginger into thin strips; slice green peppers diagonally.

4. Put red pepper powder in a strainer or meshwork ladle and stir in the flour gruel to tint it light pink. Discard the large flakes of pepper powder that remain in the strainer. Add thread green onions, garlic strips, green pepper and ginger to the gruel. Drain the salted *yŏlmu*. Dip handfuls of *yŏlmu* in the seasoned gruel and place in a container.

Note

Be gentle when you wash *yŏlmu* because it will smell if washed hard. Wash 3 or 4 times, salt lightly and drain. Do not rinse after salting because the *yŏlmu* will become bland.

You can make good *yŏlmu kimch'i* by adding young Korean cabbages to the *yŏlmu.*

To seed green peppers, roll them between the palms of your hands before cutting them lengthwise. The seeds will fall out when the peppers are opened. Don't remove the white veins inside because they are flavorful.

Yŏlmu kimch'i tastes even better if you make cucumber *kimch'i* (*oi sobaegi*) at the same time and layer the two in the same container.

Radish and Cabbage *Kimch'i*
Nabak kimch'i, 나박김치

2 cups white radish, cut into pieces
2 cups Korean cabbage, cut into pieces
$\frac{1}{4}$ *cup green onion, sliced*
$\frac{1}{2}$ *teaspoon chopped or sliced garlic*
$\frac{1}{2}$ *teaspoon sliced ginger*
2 tablespoons grated onion
2 tablespoons roasted salt
1 tablespoon sugar
1 tablespoon red pepper powder
4 cups water
minari, *if available*

1. Cut radish into $1 \times 1\frac{1}{2}$ inch rectangles $\frac{1}{16}$ inch thick to make 2 cups. Cut cabbage about the same size as the radish. Cut green onions about the same length as the radish.

2. Mix (1) with chopped or sliced garlic, sliced ginger, and grated onion. Place the mixture in the container in which it will be stored.

3. Season lukewarm water with salt and sugar and stir in red pepper powder using a strainer or meshwork ladle. Pour over the mixture in the container.

Note

Notice that the water, not the cabbage and radish, is salted. This will cause the ingredients to float rather than sink in the water. If you want to add *minari*, cut it the same length as the green onion and add after the *nabak kimch'i* has fermented a little; it will not become discolored but remain bright green.

For the sake of efficiency, you can grind onion, garlic and ginger all together in a blender.

Pickled Cucumber *Oiji,* 오이지

30 pickling cucumbers
coarse salt
water

1. Layer 30 pickling cucumbers in a container. Pour in enough water to cover and then drain off and measure. Boil that amount of water with coarse salt $\frac{1}{12}$ the amount of water. Pour the boiling water over the cucumbers. Stabilize the cucumbers with chopsticks and place a stone or other heavy object on them to prevent the cucumbers from floating.

2. After 2 days, pour out the water, leaving the cucumbers in the container. Boil the liquid and, after it has completely cooled, pour over the cucumbers. Repeat after 3 or 4 days. Keep in a cool place. The cucumbers will be fermented in a week. Store in the refrigerator.

Note

Reduce the amount of salt and water if the cucumbers are small. The salt water should taste rather bland. Don't worry if the salt water seems to barely cover the cucumbers; the liquid will increase as the cucumbers begin to ferment. Be sure to weigh down the cucumbers with a rock or something heavy.

Radish Water *Kimch'i*
Tongch'imi, 동치미

6 bundles small Korean white radishes
  (about 4 inches long)
6 tablespoons salt
6 tablespoons sugar
handful green onions
2 cloves garlic
sliced ginger (same amount as garlic)
10 to 12 cups water

1. Clean radishes, removing the hairy roots, peeling shoulders where dirt has become ingrained and cutting off the yellowed parts at the end of the leaves. Do not peel the entire radish, otherwise the liquid will become milky. Halve lengthwise if radish is thick.

2. Mix 3 tablespoons salt with 3 level tablespoons sugar. In a container, place a layer of washed radishes, sprinkle them with the salt and sugar mixture and repeat until all radishes are in the container. Top with a few slices of garlic and ginger and a handful of thin green onions. Let stand for exactly one day.

3. Just a day later, boil water with 3 tablespoons salt and 3 tablespoons sugar. When the water is still quite warm (about 100° F), pour over the radishes. It looks neater if the garlic and ginger are wrapped in gauze, because they won't get in your way when you scoop it for serving.

4. Leave at room temperature 1 or 2 days to ferment and store in the refrigerator. Peel the radish to serve. Cut the leaves to bite size and serve with the radish and plenty of liquid.

Note

The *tongch'imi* water acquires the crispy refreshing flavor only if the warm water is poured exactly 24 hours after the radishes are salted.

Popular Dishes

I have included here some popular recipes that don't seem to fall into any specific category. For example, cold bean soup *(k'ongguk)*, cold *kimch'i* soup *(kimch'i mari)*, and dumpling soup *(mandu kuk)* are not really soup, despite their names. Each of them is a substantial dish that can be a meal in itself with very few side dishes. They are specialties that you can make occasionally just for a change. However, I make cold bean soup every morning for your father-in-law because it is a good substitute for breakfast. He likes it because all he has to do is drink it up. With some fresh vegetables and fruit, it makes a very healthy breakfast.

Rice-Cake Soup   *Ttŏkkuk* , 떡국

6 cups rice cake slices
1 egg
$\frac{1}{4}$ cup sliced green onion
2 teaspoons soup soy sauce
1 teaspoon table salt

A. 1 pound beef brisket
   2 or 3 cloves garlic
   3 or 4 stalks large green onion
   8 cups water

B. $\frac{1}{4}$ pound ($\frac{1}{2}$ cup) beef
   $\frac{1}{2}$ tablespoon sugar
   $\frac{1}{2}$ tablespoon soy sauce
   1 teaspoon chopped green onion
   1 teaspoon sesame salt
   1 teaspoon chopped garlic
   1 teaspoon sesame oil
   $\frac{1}{4}$ teaspoon black pepper

1. Prepare broth by boiling (A) ingredients, first on high heat for 15 minutes, then on medium heat for 2 hours. The broth will become about 6 cups. Add soup soy sauce and salt.

2. Slice beef into thin strips, mix with (B) ingredients, and stir-fry.

3. Rinse rice cake slices and add to the broth when it is boiling hard. Bring to a boil on high heat.

4. Beat an egg and mix with a drop of sesame oil and sliced green onion.

5. When the rice cake slices have floated to the top, add the egg mixture and cover. Turn off the heat and let stand for 1 minute for the egg to cook.

6. Place in individual bowls and top the soup with fried beef strips.

Note

Pulgogi can be used to garnish the *ttŏkkuk*. Or slice beef and green onions into pencil-thick strips about 2 inches long and thread onto toothpicks, brush with *yangnyŏmjang* sauce and fry in a pan.

Instead of pouring the beaten egg into the soup, you can fry it into a thin sheet, cut into diamonds and sprinkle on top after placing the soup in serving bowls. You can also roast and shred a sheet of laver to sprinkle on top of the soup.

The reason you should rinse the rice cake slices before adding to the boiling soup is to prevent them from thickening the soup.

Cold Bean Soup   *K'ongguk,* 콩국

This is called a "soup" but it is not served with rice like other Korean soups but is drunk like milk or used as a broth for noodles. It is a popular health food because of all the talk about the virtue of vegetable protein. It is believed to be highly effective in lowering cholesterol.

1 cup soybeans
1 tablespoon roasted sesame or perilla seeds
1 teaspoon roasted salt
water

1. Wash and soak soybeans in 2 cups water for 4 to 5 hours. One cup soybeans will swell to 2 cups. Boil in 2 cups water for 5 to 6 minutes. Leave the pan uncovered so it will not boil over. The beans are ready when they are half-cooked. They will be a little hard but will taste savory, not raw. Rinse in cold water to remove the skins.

2. In a blender, grind the rinsed beans and roasted sesame or perilla seeds in 2 cups water and pass through a sieve. Salt to taste.

Note

To keep from having to boil soybeans every time you want some *k'ongguk*, boil up a lot and, after rinsing, freeze by the cupful with a cup of water in plastic bags. We used to rinse the beans thoroughly to remove all the skins but nowadays they say that the skins are healthful, so it is up to you. You can skip sieving if you grind the beans finely.

K'ongguk can also be made with black beans.

Noodles with *Kimch'i*
Pibim kuksu, 비빔국수

½ *pound noodles*
½ *pound (1 cup) ground beef*
2 *cups* **kimch'i**, *chopped*
1 *tablespoon vinegar*
pulgogi *sauce*

A. 1 tablespoon sesame oil
   1 tablespoon sesame salt
   1 tablespoon sugar

B. 1 tablespoon red pepper paste
   1 teaspoon sugar
   1 teaspoon sesame oil

C. ½ teaspoon table salt
   1 tablespoon sesame oil

1. Use *pulgogi* already cooked, or season ground beef with *pulgogi* sauce (see page 27) and stir-fry.

2. Shake stuffing from *kimch'i* and cut *kimch'i* into pieces. Mix with (A) seasoning.

3. Mix (B) ingredients.

4. Cook noodles in boiling water, rinse in cold water and drain. Mix with (C) ingredients. Add the meat and *kimch'i*. Add the seasoned red pepper paste to taste. Add vinegar at the last minute and mix again.

Dumpling Soup   *Mandu kuk,* 만둣국

1 *pound (2 cups) finely ground beef or pork*
4 *cups cabbage, chopped, or 1 cup* **kimch'i**
1 *onion*
4 *cups mung bean sprouts (optional)*
1 *pack bean curd* (**tubu**)
salt, pepper, sesame oil, sesame salt, garlic, ginger

A. 1 tablespoon soy sauce
   1 teaspoon table salt
   1 tablespoon sesame oil
   1 tablespoon chopped green onion
   ½ teaspoon black pepper
   ½ teaspoon chopped garlic
   ½ teaspoon chopped ginger

B. 3 cups flour
   ¾ cup cold water
   1 tablespoon salt
   1 tablespoon cooking oil.

1. To make *mandu* filling, season ground meat with (A) seasoning. Knead well.

2. Chop onion to make 1 cup.

3. Mash the bean curd with the back of a knife and squeeze in a cloth to wring out liquid. To 1 cup of squeezed bean curd, add 1 teaspoon salt, 1 teaspoon seasme oil and a little pepper. Mix well.

Dumpling Soup
Mandu kuk

147

4. Parboil mung bean sprouts and squeeze. Four cups fresh mung bean will become $\frac{2}{3}$ cup. Season with $\frac{1}{4}$ teaspoon table salt, $\frac{1}{2}$ teaspoon sesame oil and a little pepper.

5. If you use cabbage, mince it to make 4 cups and sprinkle with 2 tablespoons salt (1 tablespoon table salt). When the cabbage has become limp, rinse in cold water and squeeze out the water.

If you use Korean cabbage, quarter it and soak in salt water (1 tablespoon table salt in 4 cups of water) or parboil. Either way, rinse well and chop finely. Squeeze out the water; 1 cup when squeezed will be enough. *Kimch'i* is a good substitute for cabbage. Rinse, chop finely and squeeze.

You can use zucchini in place of cabbage or *kimch'i*. Cut into fine strips to make 3 cups. Sprinkle with 1 tablespoon table salt. Squeeze out the liquid until you have 1 cup.

6. When all the ingredients are ready, mix the meat with the chopped onion, the bean curd and the rest of the ingredients, in that order. Season with 1 tablespoon each of sesame oil, sesame salt and chopped garlic and 1 teaspoon pepper. Add salt to taste.

7. To make skins, make a dough with (B) ingredients. Knead well and allow to stand in a plastic bag or in a clean, wet towel. Shape the dough into a sausage-like roll, cut into chestnut size pieces and roll into thin circles.

8. Put about 1 tablespoonful of the filling at the center of a circle, fold over and crimp the edges well together.

9. Make broth and season as you ordinarily would. Bring to a boil. Add the *mandu* and when they float to the top, add $\frac{1}{2}$ cup cold water and bring to a boil again. Serve.

You can serve *mandu* in plain water rather than in broth. Boil 4 cups of water with 1 tablespoon of cooking oil and 1 tablespoon of salt. Add *mandu* and when they float to the top, add $\frac{1}{2}$ cup of cold water and bring to boil again. Serve in ice water mixed with 1 tablespoon of salt and 1 tablespoon of cooking oil. Serve with a mixture of vinegar and soy sauce for dipping.

Makes 8 servings.

Note
I use a little more meat than average. Add a little ginger juice when seasoning the meat if you are using pork.

$\frac{1}{2}$ *pound (1 cup) ground pork*
$\frac{1}{2}$ *cup chopped onion*
$\frac{1}{2}$ *cup finely cut Chinese chives* (**puch'u**)
$\frac{1}{2}$ *teaspoon salt*

A. *1 teaspoon soy sauce*
   $\frac{1}{2}$ *teaspoon salt*
   1 tablespoon chopped green onion
   1 teaspoon chopped garlic
   $\frac{1}{2}$ *teaspoon ginger juice*
   1 tablespoon sesame oil
   dash pepper

1. Season 1 cup ($\frac{1}{2}$ pound) ground pork with (A) ingredients. Mix with chopsticks whisking them in one direction only. Add chopped onion, finely cut Chinese chives (*puch'u*) and salt.

2. Make the skins the same as for Korean *mandu*.

Note

Chinese restaurant dumplings are soft and tasty because they have a lot more fat than we normally like to use. You can make the filling soft by adding a generous amount of cooking oil.

If you have made more filling than skins, cut the leaves off *kimch'i*, rinse and squeeze. Spread a leaf on the cutting board and wrap a spoonful of filling with it. Cook in anchovy broth or beef broth, and you have very good *kimch'i* rolls.

On the other hand, it is no problem if you have made more dough than the filling. Roll the leftover dough into one big circle, sprinkle it with flour, fold many times and cut into noodles. Keep in the freezer, and you can make nice noodle soup whenever you want.

For your Buddhist aunt who is a vegetarian, I use dried radish pieces (*mu mallaeng-i*) instead of meat to make the filling. It is very good and has a clean taste. Try it when you have a vegetarian guest. Soak the *mu mallaeng-i* and cook with water and soy sauce until soft to touch. Chop or mash before adding to the filling.

As for the skins, homemade ones taste better and some people would not have them otherwise, but store-bought ones are far more convenient. Fortunately, your husband likes dumplings too much to care whether the skins are homemade or bought. Bought skins will seal better if you brush the edges with egg whites. Chinese grocers have thick dumpling skins which taste like homemade ones.

Fried Dumplings
T'wigim mandu, 튀김만두

½ pound (1 cup) ground beef or pork
4 cups chopped cabbage
½ cup chopped onion
1 egg
salt, chopped garlic, black pepper, sesame salt, sesame oil

1. Chop cabbage to make 4 cups. Mix 1 cup water with *¼* cup salt (1 tablespoon table salt), sprinkle over the cabbage. Let stand for 30 minutes.

2. Mince onions.

3. Heat a pan and fry meat with 1 tablespoon soy sauce, 1 teaspoon garlic and 1 teaspoon pepper. When the meat is done, place in a large bowl and let cool. When cool, add minced onion to it.

4. When the cabbage has become soft, drain and squeeze in a sack (it will become *¾* cup). Mix with the meat and add 1 tablespoon of sesame salt and 1 tablespoon of sesame oil. Add an egg to help the ingredients stay together.

5. Wrap the above filling in *mandu* skins. You can either pan-fry or deep-fry. Because the meat is already cooked, fry just until the skins are cooked.

To pan-fry: Heat the pan, add oil and put the *mandu* in. When the skin becomes light brown, add 3 tablespoons of water, cover and reduce the heat. They are done when you can no longer hear the water sizzling and the skin has become clear. You can fry further by turning them but I wouldn't because you risk ruining the shape of the *mandu.*

Note

I am not saying how much salt you should use because the cabbage is salted. Taste the meat (it's already cooked) and if it is bland, add more salt. The *mandu* should be salty because frying will make it bland. Serve with a mixture of vinegar and soy sauce for dipping.

2 cups **kimch'i,** *sliced*
2 cups beef broth
½ cup water **kimch'i (tongch'imi)** *or* **kimch'i** *juice*
3 cups cold rice
seame oil, sugar, vinegar, sesame salt
kimch'i *juice, beef broth, rice*

A. *2 teaspoons sesame oil*
   2 teaspoons vinegar
   2 tablespoons sugar
   2 tablespoons sesame salt

1. Shake stuffing from *kimch'i* and cut into pieces; make 2 cups. Mix with (A) seasoning.

2. Mix radish water *kimch'i* or *kimch'i* juice with beef broth, season with 1 teaspoon sugar and salt to taste. Add cooled rice and *kimch'i* and season further with sesame oil, sugar and vinegar to suit your taste. Sprinkle with sesame salt and serve.

Note

This is one of the favorite snacks for northerners, especially on cold winter nights. Sometimes slices of *memil muk* (buckwheat jelly) and/or *pindaettŏk* (mung bean pancake) are added. As for the *kimch'i* juice, the juice of *tongch'imi* is the best but you can use the juice of any *kimch'i* if you don't have *tongch'imi*. Thin slices of boiled beef or pork are also good additions but only when you already have them. This is the kind of snack that everyone has their own idea how it should taste, so we don't need to try to season accurately. Just place sugar, sesame salt and vinegar on the table to make everyone happy.

You might want to try mixing very thin noodles instead of rice.

Even when the *kimch'i* is sour, a little vinegar is a must because it makes the food refreshing.

Desserts

Korean cuisine has a great array of desserts but most of them are too complicated to make at home, much less out of a cookbook. The crispy and sweet rice cookies such as *kangjŏng* and *sanja* are mouth-watering even to think about but you have to be a real expert to be able to make them. I did all kinds of Korean dishes out of cookbooks when I was bored stiff living in the Philippines away from the children, but I never was able to make decent *kangjŏng* and *sanja*. I also wasted heaps of good flour and sesame oil before I was able to fry *yakkwa* (honey cookies) just right, not so soft that they would dissolve in the oil or not so hard that biting into them was a dental hazard. I was able to make them properly only after I came back to Seoul and had proper lessons.

Remembering my frustration in those days, I have written down only those recipes that are easy and fool proof.

Flower Pancake *Hwajŏn,* 화전

1 cup glutinous rice powder
2 to 3 tablespoons boiling water
$\frac{1}{4}$ teaspoon salt
jujubes
sweet bean paste filling (**p'atso**), oil, syrup

1. Pour boiling water and salt over glutinous rice powder. Knead well. When you use bought powder, which is very dry, you will need about 6 tablespoons water, but if you are using rice powder fresh from the grinder and still wet, you will need much less, only about 2 tablespoons. Just keep in mind the dough should be a little softer than dumpling dough.

2. Roll dough into 1 inch balls, then flatten into circles 2 inches across. Grease the pan and fry, always on low heat. *Hwajŏn* will burn before they get cooked if on high heat. When they are fried, remove from the pan and pour syrup over them.

If you want to decorate, pit jujubes, flatten with a rolling pin and cut into diamond shapes. Fry one side of the *hwajŏn* well while arranging the jujube pieces in a flower shape on the top. Turn and fry briefly to make the red color of the jujube stay bright.

If you want to make stuffed *hwajŏn*, shape the dough into an oval, place the *p'atso* filling in the center and fold it.

To make syrup

$\frac{1}{2}$ cup sugar
$\frac{1}{2}$ cup water
2 tablespoons honey

Boil sugar and water on low heat. Do not stir. (The water and sugar will separate if you stir.) Remove from heat as soon as boiling begins. When it stops boiling, add honey.

1 pound sweet beans
1½ cups sugar
¼ cup honey
½ teaspoon salt

1. Boil sweet beans hard in 10 times as much water until the beans can be easily mashed with a spatula. Mash the beans and strain through a sieve to remove the skins. Discard the dredge and rinse the sieve. Strain the sieved liquid again. Pour the liquid into a cloth sack, squeeze out the water.

2. Retrieve the sediment in the sack and sauté with sugar, honey and salt. The sediment will seem dry but it becomes watery after you turn the heat off. Keep it on the fire and stir continuously. It will bubble and splash all over the place. When the splashing is over, big holes will appear here and there and steam will come out. This means that the paste is almost done. Remove from the heat before too long because, if it is kept on the heat long after the steam begins to dissipate, it will harden when cooled.

3. Keep in the freezer. It won't go bad for a long, long time.

Note

A little *p'atso* in the freezer is very convenient. In addition to *hwajŏn*, you can make glutinous rice cake Japanese style (*mochi*) with this filling. Homemade filling is much better than the canned kind you buy at the market. Japanese filling is too sweet for my taste. On the other hand, you might find this paste too bland. Add or subtract sugar to suit your taste.

White Rice Cake | *Paeksŏlgi,* 백설기

6 cups freshly ground rice powder
½ cup sugar
¼ cup honey
½ cup water
⅓ cup flour

1. Sift the rice powder. If the rice powder does not contain salt, add 1 teaspoon of table salt.

2. Boil water and sugar until the sugar dissolves. Cool and mix with rice powder and honey. Because the wetness of the freshly ground powder can differ from one miller to another, you need to adjust the water. Do not pour all of the sugar water at one time but drip in small amounts. The powder is mixed with enough water if it barely cakes when squeezed in the hand. If the powder is already wet enough to cake, do not add any water but honey and sugar only.

3. Bring water to a boil in a pan. Spread a wet cloth on a Korean earthenware or Chinese bamboo steamer, put the mixture in it and smooth the top. Cover with a wet cloth, place the steamer on the pan and steam.

4. Make dough with flour and 2 tablespoons water. Roll the dough into a long band and seal between the steamer and the pan so that the steam will not escape.

If you are using a Chinese bamboo steamer, just wet paper towels, fold them into a band and seal.

5. Steam for 30 to 40 minutes. Simmer for 5 minutes before turning the heat off.

Note

After placing the rice dough in the steamer, before steaming, pass a knife through to the bottom along the line you would want to cut the cake. This way you won't need to cut the cake after it is done. It is not so easy to cut the hot rice cake neatly because it will stick to the knife.

Rice Cake Balls *Kyŏngdan,* 경단

4 cups glutinous rice powder (fresh)
1 cup sugar
½ cup water
tangerine syrup (**yuja ch'ŏng**)
jujube
dressing powder

1. Sieve the rice powder.

2. Boil water with sugar and add to the rice powder while still hot. Knead into dough.

3. Roll the dough into balls about 1 inch across.

   If you want to fill the balls, make the filling with jujubes. Pit jujubes, chop them finely and mix with tangerine syrup.

4. Cook the balls in boiling water, rinse in cold water and roll in the dressing powder.

To make dressing powder

sweet beans
black sesame seeds
green or white beans

Sweet Bean Dressing *(P'at kŏmul)*
Make *p'atso* on page 154, but without honey. Roast *p'atso* on low heat until it is almost dry. Remove from fire and let it air dry. It is convenient if you make a big batch and keep some in the freezer.

To use, wet 3 cups *p'atso* powder with 1 cup water boiled with ½ cup sugar. Pass through a sieve.

Black Sesame Dressing *(Hŭgimja)*
Wash black sesame, drain in a sieve. Roast, being careful not to burn. Grind finely in a mortar or blender and sieve.

Bean Powder *(K'ong karu)*
Wash green or white beans and roast in a frying pan. Do not burn. Spread beans on a tray and roll with a rolling pin to remove the skin from the beans. Winnow the skins away. Add a pinch of salt and grind the beans finely. Sieve.

4 cups glutinous rice
2 cups chestnuts
2 tablespoons brown sugar
2 tablespoons white sugar
2 cups jujubes
2 tablespoons pine nuts

A. 4 tablespoons sesame oil
   4 tablespoons soy sauce
   5 tablespoons honey
   6 tablespoons brown sugar
   6 tablespoons white sugar

1. Soak rice in water for 6 to 7 hours; 4 cups rice will swell to 6 to 7 cups.

2. Place a hemp cloth at the bottom of the steamer and steam the rice on it.

3. Peel the chestnuts and boil in $\frac{1}{2}$ cup water. Add brown sugar and white sugar and simmer until almost all the water has evaporated.

4. Pit jujubes and cut into 3 or 4 pieces. Boil the pits in water about three times the pits. When the flesh remaining on the pits is well cooked, pass through a strainer, pressing with a spoon. There should be about $\frac{1}{2}$ cup of liquid.

5. Place the steamed rice in a large bowl, add the mixture of (A) ingredients and mix well. Add pine nuts, chestnuts jujube pieces and jujube liquid and mix again.

6. Place the entire mixture in a container and cover with a lid or with cooking foil. Place the container in a pot with a little water and heat for 6 to 8 hours.

Note

Yakshik looks and tastes best and has a lingering flavor when cooked in the traditional way as explained here. However, if you think this takes too much time, try the following with a pressure cooker.

1. Soak 4 cups glutinous rice.

2. Mix rice well with 1 cup brown sugar, 2 cups water, 3 tablespoons soy sauce, 3 tablespoons sesame oil, and 5 tablespoons honey.

3. Add 2 cups chestnuts and 2 cups jujubes.

4. Cover and cook until the pressure regulator rattles. Lower the heat to medium and cook for 2 minutes; lower the heat more and cook for 1 minute; simmer at the lowest heat for 1 minute; and remove from heat.

Pine Needle Rice Cake *Songp'yŏn,* 송편

3 cups freshly powdered rice flour
½ cup sugar water
sesame oil
salt
pine needles

filling :
   mung beans
   green beans
   sesame seeds
   jujubes
   chestnuts

(Make sure that salt is added when the rice gets powdered at the mill, *ttŏkpang-agan.*)

1. Rub rice powder with hands and pass through a sieve.

2. Mix the powder with boiling water sweetened at the rate of 1 part sugar to 6 parts water. Knead for a long time into dough and let stand wrapped in a wet cloth.

3. Make a ball out of a small piece of the dough, shape it into a circle in the palm of your hand, fill with filling and shape. (Squeeze the dough to eliminate air from the filling to prevent the cake from opening while steaming.) Repeat until all the dough and/or filling is gone. Usually 1 cup rice powder will yield 8 pieces of *songp'yŏn.*

4. Spread pine needles, well rinsed and drained, on the bottom of the steamer. Place the *songp'yŏn* on the pine needles and steam 40 minutes. If pine needles are not available, use a piece of cloth.

5. When the *songp'yŏn* is cooked, rinse and brush with sesame oil and salt. Or add ½ tablespoon table salt and ½ tablespoon sesame oil to 2 cups water and rinse *songp'yŏn* in it.

To make filling
Songp'yŏn is usually filled with sweetened sesame seeds, chestnuts, beans and many other things.

Sesame seed filling

Mix 2 tablespoons well-roasted sesame seeds with 1 tablespoon sugar, 1 teaspoon honey and a little salt.

Chestnut filling

Cut cooked chestnuts into pieces the size of beans to make $\frac{1}{2}$ cup and mix with 1 tablespoon honey, and 1 teaspoon sugar. Simmer and add $\frac{1}{2}$ teaspoon cinnamon powder. Mix again.

Sometimes I drain canned chestnuts, flavor them with cinnamon and mash. I don't add sugar because the chestnuts are already sweet.

Jujube filling

Pit jujubes and chop finely. To 2 tablespoons chopped jujube, add 1 teaspoon sugar and $\frac{1}{2}$ teaspoon honey. Mix well.

Mung bean filling

Soak split mung beans and thoroughly remove the skins. Steam the beans until they are completely cooked. To 1 cup cooked mung beans, add $\frac{1}{4}$ cup sugar and $\frac{1}{2}$ teaspoon salt. Mix well.

Twisted Cookies *Maejagwa,* 매자과

3 cups flour
1 tablespoon cooking oil
$\frac{3}{4}$ cup water
1 tablespoon sugar
1 teaspoon ginger juice
1 teaspoon salt
oil for frying
pine nut powder

1. Pour cooking oil over flour and mix thoroughly by rubbing between your palms. Mix with water, sugar, ginger juice and salt. Knead well.

2. When the dough is smooth, roll it out into thin sheets and cut them into about 1 × 2 inch rectangles. Slit each at the center without slitting to the ends. Pull one end of each piece through the slit to make a ribbon-like twist.

3. Deep-fry on low heat (about 270° F, otherwise they will burn before they are cooked) and soak in syrup (see page 153 to make syrup). Sprinkle with pine nut powder before serving.

Sweet Rice Drink *Shik'ye,* 식혜

2 cups malt powder (**yŏtkirŭm**)
2 cups glutinous rice or plain rice
lemon or ginger juice
pine nuts

1. Soak powdered malt in 5 cups of water and let stand for about 15 minutes. Strain the malt-water through a fine sieve. Remove the malt remaining in the sieve into a bowl, rub hard in an additional cup of water and strain again through the sieve. Sieve again if the strained water has any bits floating in it. Let stand to allow the malt-water to settle.

2. Cook rice using less water than usual to make it very crispy. Place the hot rice in an electric rice cooker and pour only the clear malt-water on top over the rice. Let stand for 6~7 hours at "keep warm" until rice begins to float to the top. If you don't have a rice cooker, use a steamer keeping it at 250°F. When about ten grains of rice have floated, rub one between your fingers. If the grain is not sticky, it has fermented well.

3. Take out about half of the fermented rice, rinse through a strainer, put in a container with enough water to cover and keep in the refrigerator.

4. Bring the malt-water to a hard boil and then strain again. Let cool and store in the refrigerator. To serve, place in bowls, add $\frac{1}{2}$ teaspoon ginger or lemon juice, and sprinkle with the rinsed, fermented rice and pine nuts.

Note
The rice drink becomes quite sweet without sugar if you use enough of the malt. Be sure to use only the clear malt-water on top. You would think the sediment would make it sweeter but it doesn't help at all. It just makes the drink dark and heavy.

Watermelon Punch
Subak hwach'ae, 수박화채

watermelon
honey

1. Cut off the top of the watermelon (in a circle) and keep for a lid. Poke the flesh with a long chopstick many times to make tunnels for the honey to run through. Pour honey into the holes, put the top on, and cover with a wet paper. (Adjust the amount of honey to taste.)

2. Place the watermelon in a double boiler or, if you don't have one large enough to hold it, in a pan and put the pan in a second pan with boiling water in it and simmer for 1 hour.1

3. Let cool and keep in the refrigerator before serving.

Note

Professor Kang In-hi, a great expert in the royal cuisine of the Chosŏn Dynasty (1392-1910), found this recipe in an ancient document. She vows it is good even for those allergic to watermelon and for little babies.

Dinner Guests

From the beginning of our marriage, our house was often full of people. We loved to have our friends around and at our urging they usually stayed for dinner. My sister, who lived next door, was a great cook, and all I had to do was set the table and do the dishes afterward. Life became quite tough after she moved to the States. I had to do all the cooking but however hard I tried, the food did not turn out like my sister's. Above all, I was perpetually short of time because I was working at that time. How I regretted that I had not learned to cook properly! I had not cared enough and my sister was an impatient teacher who would rather do everything herself than be bothered so often with stupid questions when she was busy cooking. Nevertheless, I had received basic training from my sister, and I started working from that. Experience was the best teacher after all.

We tend to make too much or too little when we have dinner guests. According to my experience, we need about 12 ounces of food including rice and soup for each guest. Strapping young persons with a good appetite and Americans sometimes need up to 1 pound each. Generally, there will be enough food if you prepare one kind of food on an ordinary sized dish for each of your guests.

It is a good idea to write down what you cooked for whom and what was the favorite of each guest.

It will be very helpful when you have him or her for dinner again. Dinner preparation is half done if you have decided the menu according to your budget and to their preferences, and shopped and cleaned the ingredients.

A basic menu includes an appetizer, a fresh and a cooked vegetable, a stewed meat or fish (*tchim*), a roasted meat (*kui*), a pan-fried food (*chŏnya*), a soup, rice, tea and fruit. The kind of dishes should be increased with the number of people you are going to entertain. Westerners seem to like a generous main dish rather than a little of everything whereas it is the other way around with Koreans. It does not make much difference in terms of time whether you make a great deal of one thing or a little of various things. The latter of course takes more time but not really that much. An assortment of fresh vegetables, a cooked vegetable, a *chŏnya*, a *kui* and a main dish and soup will be more than enough for a lunch.

It will save time if you organize the groceries by kind such as vegetables, seasoning, meat and seafood and cut, chop and slice them in an order that will require you to wash the cutting board a minimum number of times. It saves even more time and effort if you already have the green onions, garlic and ginger chopped and kept in the refrigerator.

It is also very helpful when you have to cook on short notice if you keep meat cut or sliced and labelled according to kind and use. Better decide in advance which recipe takes more time and which one less. If you are to make soup and vegetable dishes, for example, begin with the soup and while it is on the stove, deal with the vegetables.

I always make a list of dishes I am going to serve and stick it somewhere I can see it easily. If I don't, I sometimes find one or two dishes I forgot to serve after the dinner is over and the guests are all gone.

I have a basic menu when I entertain our Western friends: mung bean pancakes (*pindaettŏk*), mixed vegetables (*chapch'ae*), broiled beef (*pulgogi*), fried pork ribs (*toeji kalbi kangjŏng*) or chicken (*tak kangjŏng*) plus some other dishes. These dishes are universally popular. Besides, the *chapch'ae*, *pulgogi* and *kimch'i* are representative of Korean food.

When you have an unexpected visitor near meal time, and you have nothing prepared, first begin with rice. Electric rice cookers take too much time when you are in a hurry. Cook in a pan. When you are cooking 4 cups of rice, for example, heat 5 cups of water in a pan and when the water begins to boil, pour in the rinsed rice and stir. Cover and lower the heat. When the water has almost all disappeared, lower the heat even more and simmer 5 minutes. Serve about 10 minutes after the rice is removed from the stove. The amount of the water should be increased or decreased a little depending on how long the rice has been soaked.

The following is a list of food by kind that you could consider when preparing a formal dinner.

Choose one or two from each of the following categories.

Appetizers

Mustard salad (*kyŏjach'ae*), nine-section dish (*kujŏlp'an*), pressed meat (*p'yŏnyuk*), sweet meat (*changsanjŏk*), fried dumplings (*twigim mandu*)

Hot Vegetables

Mixed vegetables (*chapch'ae*), green pepper or bell pepper *chapch'ae*, sautéed bellflower roots (*toraji*), bracken shoots (*kosari*), cucumber or zucchini

Cold Vegetables

Spinach, white radish strips (*mu saengch'ae*), stuffed cucumber (*oi sŏn*), acorn or buckwheat jelly (*muk*)

Stewed Food (*Tchim*)

Rib stew (*kalbi tchim*), sweet chicken (*tak kangjŏng*), fried fish (*saengsŏn tchim*), teriyaki (*tak chorim, Japanese style*), shrimp *tchim*, dried pollack *tchim*, bean curd *tchim*

Broiled Food

Broiled beef *(pulgogi)*, beef ribs, pork ribs, fish

Pan-fried Food (*Chŏnya*)

Mung bean pancakes (*pindaettŏk*), meat patties (*ton chŏn*), beef fillets (*kogi chŏn*), fish fillets (*saengsŏn chŏn*), stuffed green peppers (*koch'u chŏn*), shrimp (*saeu chŏn*), oyster and green onion (*kulp'a chŏn*), crab meat (*kyesal chŏn*), fried bean curd (*tubu puch'im*)

Soup

Fancy hot pot (*shinsŏllo*), vegetable soup (*yach'ae kuk*), dumpling soup (*mandu kuk*)

Others

Laver rolls (*kim pap*), fried rice (*pokkŭm pap*), dumplings (*mandu*), rice mixed with vegetables (*pibim pap*), rice mixed with *kimch'i* (*kimch'i pap*), cold noodles (*naengmyŏn*)

Desserts

Fruit, tea

Mustard Salad *Kyŏjach'ae,* 겨자채

2 cups jellyfish (**haep'ari**)
1 cup cucumber strips
$\frac{1}{2}$ cup carrot strips
15 medium shrimp
$\frac{1}{8}$ cup boiled beef strips
1 Korean pear
beer
mustard sauce (page 29)

A. 1 tablespoon chopped garlic
   1 tablespoon vinegar
   3 tablespoons sugar
   3 tablespoons water

B. 1 teaspoon vinegar
   1 teaspoon sugar
   3 tablespoons water
   dash salt

1. Soak jellyfish in cold water to remove salt. The water should be changed several times until the jellyfish is free of salt and becomes tender. If you buy jellyfish already sliced into strips, cut into bite-size lengths. If you have to slice it yourself, cut into 2-inch lengths first, then slice into strips, and soak in cold water. When the jellyfish tastes bland, dip it briefly in boiling water. It will shrink a great deal. Rinse in cold water. Blend (A) ingredients well and pour over the jellyfish. It will become soft again.

2. Cut cucumber and carrot into thin, 2-inch-long strips.

3. Cut boiled beef into strips the same as the cucumber and carrot.

4. Peel a pear and cut into thin strips.

5. Skewer 15 unshelled shrimps with tooth picks lengthwise to prevent curling. Boil in beer and a dash of salt for 5 minutes. When they are cooked, remove the shells and soak in a mixture of (B) ingredients.

6. When all the ingredients are ready, mix them with the mustard sauce (page 29) to taste.

167

Note

You don't need to use all the vegetables. You can make salad with what you have. Scalded mung bean sprouts, their seeds and hairy ends removed, are a good addition. Shredded *matsal* (artificial crab made of ground fish) is also nice for its flavor and color. When you don't have a pear, use white radish strips instead.

Nine-Section Dish *Kujolp'an,* 구절판

¼ pound lean beef
5 oak mushrooms (p'yogo)
1 cup carrot strips
1 cup cucumber strips
1 cup white radish strips
½ cup green pepper strips
2 eggs
2 tablespoons **pulgogi** *sauce (page 27)*
salt
pine nut powder

1. Slice beef along the grain into fine strips. Season with *pulgogi* sauce and stir-fry. Allow to cool.

2. Soak mushrooms. Drain and slice into thin strips. Strain *pulgogi* sauce through a sieve and season the mushroom with the liquid. Stir-fry.

3. Cut carrot, cucumber (do not use seedy inside) and white radish into thin strips about 2 inches long. Sprinkle each with 1 teaspoon salt, squeeze when limp. Stir-fry separately.

4. Cut green peppers into thin strips like the other vegetables and stir-fry with 1 teaspoon salt.

5. Separate 2 eggs. Fry the yolks and whites separately in very thin layers on a lightly greased pan. Cut into fine strips the same length as the vegetables.

6. When all eight ingredients are prepared, arrange each in one of the eight side compartments of the nine-section dish minding the contrast of colors.

To make the crepes to go in the central section

1 cup flour
1 cup water
½ teaspoon salt

1. Mix ingredients. Beat thoroughly and let stand for 1 hour, then pass through a sieve. Pour oil on a hot pan, then wipe out the oil with a paper towel. Turn the heat to low. Drop the batter by spoonfuls to make very thin crepes about 3 to 4 inches across. (They should be just a little smaller than the compartment they are to go in.)

2. Layer the crepes in the compartment, sprinkling pine nut powder between the layers. If you don't have pine nut powder, place a garland chrysanthemum or celery leaf on each sheet to prevent the crepes from sticking together.

Nine-Section Dish
Kujolp'an

Note

Frying the crepes is no easy task. Some suggest you need to beat an egg in the batter and others say starch should be added but it won't work that way. You don't need anything other than water and salt. The point is to let the batter stand so that it becomes glutinous.

Nowadays, some restaurants substitute very thin cuts of radish, soaked in salty, sweet, vinegar water for the crepes. It certainly is simpler to prepare but is much less tasty.

Nine-section dish is colorful and eye-catching. To eat, you put a little of everything on the crepe and fold it up. Other vegetables can be substituted.

Stuffed Cucumbers *Oisŏn,* 오이선

10 cucumbers
$\frac{1}{4}$ pound ($\frac{1}{2}$ cup) beef strips
3 oak mushrooms
2 eggs
a pinch red pepper thread
3 tablespoons **pulgogi** sauce (page 27)
sesame oil

Sauce
    3 tablespoons vinegar
    2 tablespoons water
    3 tablespoons sugar
    $\frac{1}{2}$ teaspoon table salt
    1 tablespoon prepared mustard

1. Cut cucumbers into $1\frac{1}{2}$ inch long chunks and halve them lengthwise. Soak in salty water. When cucumbers become a little soft, cut 2 or 3 slits across on the skin side and soak in the salty water again. When they have wilted, wrap in a cloth and press with a heavy weight so that the cucumbers will drain and become crisp.

2. Pour a little sesame oil on the pan and fry the cucumbers quickly. Let cool.

3. Prepare beef strips, oak mushrooms and egg strips separately as you would for *kujŏlp'an* (nine-section dish).

4. Stuff the slits in the cucumbers with beef, mushroom, egg strips and red pepper threads.

5. Make sauce by mixing the sauce ingredients.

6. About 1 hour before serving, pour the sauce over the stuffed cucumbers and drain before serving.

Note
Because this is not a main dish, about 2 or 3 cucumber pieces for each person will be enough, but the visual effect is quite impressive.

Fancy Hot Pot or Hot Pot of Various Things
Shinsŏllo, 신선로

The larger of the two *shinsŏllo* pots is for 4 persons and the smaller is for 1 person. The ingredients here are for 4 persons.

10 ounces beef, tenderloin or sirloin
5 ounces fish fillets
5 inch × 5 inch tripe (ch'ŏnyŏp)
2 inch chunk white radish
½ onion
½ carrot
15 stalks minari
2 very large or 4 medium size oak mushrooms (p'yogo)
5 stone mushrooms (sŏgi)
4 eggs
½ cup flour
1 tablespoon bean curd
2 walnuts
¼ cup pine nuts

12 ginkgo nuts

Soy sauce, soup soy sauce, green onion, garlic, ginger, sesame oil, sesame salt, pepper, sugar

1. Make sauce with 2 teaspoons soy sauce, ½ teaspoon sugar, 1 teaspoon chopped green onion, 1 teaspoon sesame oil, 1 teaspoon sesame salt, and ½ teaspoon chopped garlic.

2. Cut 3 ounces beef into ⅛-inch-thick pieces. Score and marinate in the sauce. After awhile, make *chŏnya* with them by first dredging in flour, dipping in beaten egg and pan-frying over low heat.

3. Cut 5 ounces of beef into small pieces (will make about ¾ cup); slice onion. Mix the beef and onion with 1 tablespoon soy sauce, 1 teaspoon soup soy sauce, ½ teaspoon sesame oil, ½ teaspoon sugar and a pinch of pepper. Place the mixture at the bottom of the *shinsŏllo* pot.

4. Mince about 1 tablespoonful of beef and mix with 1 tablespoon crushed bean curd. Season like the beef and onion mixture (3) and roll into about 20 little balls. Dredge in flour, dip in beaten egg and pan-fry, being careful not to flatten them into patties.

5. Make *chŏnya* with the fish fillets as you did with the beef (2). Before frying, sprinkle the fish with salt and pepper. When you use frozen fish, thaw in cold water diluted with 1 tablespoon of coarse salt for 1 cup of water. Drain and sprinkle with pepper. To make *chŏnya*, always dredge in flour and then dip in beaten egg before frying.

6. One palm size piece of tripe is enough for one 4-person pot. To clean, dredge the tripe in a generous amount of flour, rub well and rinse in cold water; sprinkle with coarse salt, rub and rinse; then scald in salt water and rub between your palms to remove the dark skin. Season with a pinch of salt, pepper and ginger juice and knead to help the seasoning to penetrate into the tripe. Now, it is ready to be made into *chŏnya*. Dredge in flour, dip in beaten egg whites only to make white *chŏnya*.

7. Remove leafy ends of *minari*. Cut the stems into 3-inch lengths and pierce all onto a skewer, dip in flour and egg and pan-fry. (The skewer should be removed later when the *chŏnya* is to be cut to size.)

8. Separate 4 eggs and fry the yolks and half of the whites separately in thin sheets.

9. Soak *p'yogo* mushrooms in warm water for about 20 minutes and when soft, cut into pieces to fit into the pot. Season with a little soy sauce, sugar and sesame oil. Stir-fry lightly.

10. Soak *sŏgi* mushrooms in hot water, remove stems and rinse until water runs clean. Drain completely and chop up very fine. It will become about 1 teaspoon. Mix with egg whites left from (8) and fry in a thin sheet.

11. Cut carrot into thin rectangles to fit in the pot. Parboil the slices.

12. Soak 2 whole walnuts or 8 quartered ones in hot water for awhile and peel off the skins.

13. Fry shelled gingko nuts in a very little oil on low heat just long enough to turn green, sprinkle with salt and peel off the skins.

14. Make broth by boiling the remaining beef, a piece of radish, mushroom stems, left over carrot pieces and other vegetables.

15. Now, cut the beef, tripe and fish *chŏnya*, fried eggs, fried stone mushroom and other vegetables into pieces that will fit into the pot. Arrange them by color in spoke fashion in the pot and garnish with walnuts, pine nuts and gingko nuts. Pour the broth over them and serve with the lamp burning in the fire chamber.

Fancy Hot Pot or Hot Pot of Various Things
Shinsŏllo

175

Note

Shinsŏllo is a special dish served in a special pot with a fluted cylinder at the center in which a fire burns to keep the food piping hot throughout. *Shinsŏllo*, which refers to both the pot and the food in the pot, literally means a "Taoist Immortal's Brazier," a very apt name in that it is so delicious, eye-pleasing, and arduous to make — fit for a Taoist immortal no less. It is made on very special occasions only. However, just for those occasions when you are challenged to make it, here are some tips.

1. You need 4 eggs for each 4-person pot. Separate them into yolks and whites. Fry 4 sheets of yolk, each about 2 spoonfuls. Repeat with the whites. Then fry stone mushroom and egg whites, then tripe and egg whites. Combine leftover yolks and whites to coat and fry beef, fish and *minari chŏnya*.

2. When you beat eggs, beat with chopsticks, making sure they scrape the bottom of the vessel not to get too much froth. Pass through a strainer so that the egg will coat the dredged ingredients evenly.

3. Eggs should always be salted a little. The beaten egg will become brighter when fried if allowed to stand for awhile.

4. For best looking *chŏnya*, heat the pan before adding the oil. Fry over low heat and turn the pieces just once.

5. You need 1 teaspoon of flour for 2 tablespoons of ground meat to make meat balls. Spread the flour on a plate, roll the meat balls in it by shaking the plate. (One of my friends says she puts the flour in a plastic container, adds the meatballs and shakes a little because she would have flour all over the floor if she used a plate. Not a bad idea!) Dip in the egg batter and spoon out with a mesh scoop to fry. Shaking the pan itself is easier to roll the balls to fry all around.

6. You can make the best broth for *shinsŏllo* with leftover ingredients. Use the water in which oak mushrooms were soaked. It has a good flavor. Boil the mushroom stems also. Make 2 cups. You need 1 cup to fill a 4-person pot but want to have 1 extra cup to refill it.

To be practical, here is a far simpler version of *shinsŏllo* for us mortals

Make *chŏnya* with beef and fish fillets as in (2) and (5). Cut beef into small pieces, mix with onion slices and season with soy sauce, sesame oil, pepper, chopped green onion.

Place the beef and onion mixture at the bottom of the pot and cover it with beef and fish *chŏnya*, cut neatly to fit into the pot. Garnish with oak mushroom slices, strips of egg yolks and whites, green peppers, red peppers, pine nuts and gingko nuts. Pour the broth into the pot.

Steamed Fish *Saengsŏn tchim,* 생선찜

$\frac{1}{4}$ *pound ($\frac{1}{2}$ cup) beef strips*
12 palm size fillets of fish
2 cups Korean white radish strips
$\frac{1}{4}$ *cup carrot strips*
3 oak mushrooms
1 bundle **minari**
3 green peppers
3 eggs
3 tablespoons flour
$\frac{1}{2}$ *teaspoon ginger juice*
soy sauce, chopped garlic, salt, pepper, sesame oil

1. Soak fish fillets in salt water (2 teaspoons table salt to 1 cup water). Drain and sprinkle with pepper.

2. Cut beef into thin strips, season with 2 teaspoons soy sauce, 1 teaspoon chopped garlic, a dash pepper and 1 teaspoon sesame oil.

3. Soak oak mushrooms and cut into thin slices. Season with a little soy sauce, sesame oil and sugar.

4. Cut radish into strips and sprinkle with 1 teaspoon table salt. When the radish becomes tender, mix with a little sesame oil, a pinch of red pepper thread, and $\frac{1}{2}$ teaspoon ginger juice.

5. Cut carrots into strips and sprinkle with $\frac{1}{2}$ teaspoon salt.

6. Seed green peppers and cut into thin strips.

7. Mix beef (2) and radish (4) and place half of the mixture at the bottom of a bowl. Dredge the fish fillets in flour and layer half of them on the beef-radish mixture. Brush beaten egg over the fillets. Layer the remaining beef-radish mixture over the fish and then top with the remaining fish. Brush beaten egg over the fish. Garnish with carrot, mushroom, green pepper or *minari* and egg strips. Steam on a steamer rack.

8. Make 2 cups broth by boiling leftover vegetables and mushrooms. Season with soy sauce or salt. Pour on the steamed fish and serve.

Note

Frozen fish tastes almost as good as fresh if brushed with sesame oil after being sprinkled with salt and pepper.

You don't have to use all of the above ingredients for garnishing. Things that are easy to prepare or are already prepared will be enough. I usually do this recipe instead of *saengsŏn chŏnya* (fried fish fillets) when I make *chapch'ae* (mixed vegetables) because I can "borrow" some of the *chapch'ae* vegetables to garnish the fish colorfully, thus eliminating the need to cut vegetables specifically to garnish the fish.

Food for Babies

Last summer was wonderful because we had you and your children with us. Hye-jun was a real sweetie pie and Yon-jun at seven months was already teething and crawling. The little thing definitely seemed to understand me when I talked to her. It made me really happy because she ate the vegetable and beef porridge I made for her. Just like her daddy when he was that little. She liked fish porridge too and even the bread porridge which I whipped up on the spot because I didn't have any groceries at home. Like father, like daughter. I made those kinds of porridge with the same ingredients and in the same way I did for her daddy 30 years ago, and she ate with just the same relish he did.

I am very happy and thankful because you always try to make baby food yourself with fresh ingredients rather than buying ready-made ones stacked on every supermarket shelf. I must compliment your mother for your good upbringing. I am also very proud of you because you began to do so because you wanted to before I even suggested it.

Children who are exposed to a variety of food when small grow up healthy and do not become unbearably picky adults with so many likes and dislikes in their eating habits. I know you have already become an expert in making baby food, but cooking three meals a day, day in and day out, there are moments when your mind goes completely blank and you can't think of what to make for the next meal. For such occasions, I wrote down some of the kinds of porridge I used to make for your husband when he was small.

2 tablespoons rice soaked 1 hour
$\frac{1}{4}$ pound ($\frac{1}{2}$ cup) beef
$\frac{1}{4}$ carrot
$\frac{1}{4}$ onion
2 or 3 leaves spinach
$\frac{1}{2}$ potato
2 leaves cabbage
$\frac{1}{2}$ zucchini
1 tablespoon anchovy powder

(You don't need all of these at one time – about five will be enough.)

1. Boil beef in 8 cups water, skimming off the froth.

2. Add vegetables, cut into $\frac{1}{2}$ inch square pieces. Add anchovy powder or dry anchovy, cleaned of innards and crushed to pieces. When the vegetables are soft to the touch, add rice. If the rice makes the porridge too thick, add more water.

The porridge is done when the rice becomes shapeless. Crush vegetables and rice. It can be used as is, but I used to add a drop of soup soy sauce for flavoring.

Note

When my baby was 4 months old, I boiled only vegetables without the rice and beef, and passed them through a sieve and used the juice.

For about 7 months, I just crushed the vegetables in the porridge. For babies before teething, pass the porridge through a sieve.

Vegetable porridge is good in preventing constipation in a baby. According to my experience, 2 tablespoons of rice makes enough porridge for two or three feedings.

There wasn't any celery or bell peppers in my time. I think those kinds of vegetables are a good addition.

Fish Porridge *Saengsŏn chuk,* 생선죽

Fillet of white fish, rice

Boil a fillet about the size of your palm in 4 cups water and add 1 tablespoon soaked rice. Boil until the rice becomes shapeless.

Note

When the fish has bones, take it out of the water with a mesh scoop and pick out the bones with your fingers before adding the rice. Be absolutely sure there are no bones in the porridge.

Bread Porridge *Ppang chuk,* 빵죽

1 slice of bread
1 cup milk

Toast bread, break into pieces and boil in milk. This is a real quickie. I used to make it when I was pressed for time.

Chestnut Porridge *Pam chuk,* 밤죽

5 roasted chestnuts
2 tablespoons rice
8 cups water

Slit the top part of chestnuts and roast. Peel and crush them and boil in water with the soaked rice.

Chestnut porridge fattens babies up. Nowadays, what with weight watching and the fitness craze, it seems even babies should not be overweight. In the old days when I was raising children, babies were thought to be healthy babies only if they were chubby. Chestnut porridge is good for skinny babies.

Note

Be sure to roast the chestnuts before making them into porridge. My mother used to warn me time and again that porridge made with raw chestnut would give a baby indigestion.

Another bit of wisdom my mother taught me: When your baby has a cough, cut out the top of a small pumpkin and remove the seeds. Or cut out the core of a pear without cutting the bottom. Pour honey into the hollow, close with the top that was cut off. Place the pumpkin or pear in a bowl and steam for 3 or 4 hours. Strain or squeeze in a cloth. The juice works for coughs in most cases.

Food for Special Days

Life after all is about birth, aging, illness and death. It is woven around landmark occasions such as coming of age, marriages, funerals and memorial rites, or so I was taught when I was growing up. Going through these landmarks of your life, you grow up and develop thoughts and views on life quite different from those you had when you were young and unmarried.

Aside from the development of a philosophical view or religious understanding of life, the most immediate and practical issue a housewife faces on these occasions is preparation of appropriate food. These days more and more people tend to hire cooks or caterers for such days. It is a matter of family tradition, I guess, so I am writing down how we do things in our family. You would learn our ways naturally if we lived and worked together to prepare for important occasions. Living as we do, you and your families in the United States and your father-in-law and I here in Seoul, I think it is quite meaningful to put it down in writing.

September 5 is your grandmother's memorial day. This year it was a good day for all the family and relatives to get together because it fell on a Sunday. Besides, the weather was just beautiful. Traditionally, a memorial rite should be held on the day before the deceased actually died, so we should really observe your grandmother's anniversary the night of September 4 and not the 5th, but we did it on the 5th because Catholics hold memorial rites for the deceased on the day of his or her death. Anyway, we did go to mass for Grandma on the evening of the 4th and all of us including your aunt and her family in Shihŭng came over to my house and stayed overnight.

It was quite late — almost 10:00 in the evening — when everyone arrived home, but we started making *naengmyŏn* noodles and ate it with *pulgogi* barbecue. Your father-in-law was quite excited, saying that it reminded him of the old days when he was a boy and the entire clan gathered together on every memorial day. There were more than 20 of us, and it was quite a job to prepare breakfast the next morning. Everybody had a different idea for breakfast. To make everyone happy, I told them to make a list of things they wanted to have and prepared all of them: rice and soup, steamed bread, steamed dumplings, noodles and whatever else was on the list.

It was just like when I was little. In my mother's house anybody could come and sit at the table to eat whatever he or she liked. My mother always said that the best time of your life is when your house is full of visitors. The same philosophy holds in my in-law's house and also in my house.

We began to prepare food offerings right after breakfast. It was finished in good time because everyone pitched in. Besides, I had already done much of the basic preparation in advance. I did the grocery shopping and cleaned the vegetables the day before. I bought fish three days in advance, salted and let it dry in the refrigerator. Beans were also soaked in advance and made into curd (*tubu*) on the day. Homemade *tubu* is far more flavorful.

As for the food to go on the offering table, we prepared mung bean pancakes (*pindaettŏk*), meat patties (*ton chŏn*), pan-fried fish fillet (*saengsŏn chŏn*), pan-fried bean curd (*tubu chŏn*), broiled beef (*sanjŏk*), broiled chicken (*takkogi chŏk*), broiled fish (*saengsŏn chŏk*), boiled pork (*toeji kogi p'yŏnyuk*), stewed dried pollack (*pugŏ tchim*), sautéed vegetables in three colors (bracken shoots, bellflower roots, spinach), radish soup, fermented rice drink (*shik'ye*), and radish and cabbage kimch'i (*nabak kimch'i*). These are not exactly in accord with the menu prescribed by the traditional norm for ancestral rites, but they were Grandmother's favorite food. I added beef rib stew (*kalbi tchim*) and mustard salad (*kyŏjach'ae*) for the family because everyone wanted them. We are not supposed to use spicy condiments such as green onions, garlic, ginger and red pepper powder in food for memorial rites but I used them all anyway because I wanted my food to taste good.

Sanjŏk and chŏnya should all be extra-large so that they can be easily layered on the ritual plates. For the beef sanjŏk, I cut thick chunks of tenderloin and spread them to the size of a large notebook. It was quite popular, everyone commenting that it was a Korean version of tenderloin steak. I had marinated it in pulgogi sauce a couple of hours before broiling. It turned out very tender. I broiled it medium well, worrying a little bit that my maid — a perfectionist who must take a bath to cleanse herself before preparing food offerings — would raise a fuss, but she approved of the idea that meat should not be well done for memorial rites.

The chicken was opened and beaten flat with a rolling pin before broiled in yangnyŏmjang sauce. The fish was half dried and broiled in yangnyŏmjang sauce. I did not score it because, well, it was not supposed to be scored. Fruits of the season should also go on the offering table. I added fresh jujubes from the garden which I had kept in the refrigerator for this occasion.

Confucian tradition calls for the memorial rite to be held at midnight — so that the spirit can be invoked — but we said a Catholic prayer for the dead early in the evening and partook of the food because everyone had to go home and get ready for the next day. People have offices and schools to go to.

Formalities are not really that important. The real purpose of a memorial rite is to have all the family members get together to remember the deceased, renew family love and reconfirm our belief that we will all get together again over there. You were not with us this time, but I am sure you remembered your grandmother with us.

In the old days when child mortality was very high, an infant often died in the first 3 months. Parents breathed a sigh of relief when the baby became 100 days old. I guess that is why they celebrated *paegil* (100th Day) with so much ado. These days people seem to celebrate it because babies are so cute by that time. It is about this time that a baby can hold up its head properly for a studio photograph, even though it seems today's babies are so clever that they can hold their heads up from the day they are born.

It is said on a baby's *paegil* (100th Day), *paeksŏlgi* white rice cake should be made and given to 100 persons (the Korean word for "100" and for "white" are both pronounced *paek* or *paeg*). Better still, it should be made with rice donated from 100 houses, which is a task nigh impossible these days. I think a *paegil* party is a good idea for the mother to get together with her friends and relatives whom she could not meet for a long time because of the child birth and for them to congratulate her and meet her baby.

Food for the occasion includes white rice (with no other grain), *miyŏk* (seaweed) soup, *paeksŏlgi* cake, various kinds of *kui* (roast or barbecue), sautéed vegetables, *shik'ye* (fermented rice drink), and *kimch'i*. On Yon-jun's 100th day, besides the basic rice, soup, rice cake, and *shik'ye*, we made mustard salad (*kyŏjach'ae*), mixed vegetables (*chapch'ae*), and acorn jelly for vegetables, beef barbecue for *kui*, and pork ribs (*toeji kalbi kangjŏng*) and chicken in sauce (*tak p'yŏnyuk*) for *tchim*.

The First Birthday

On the first birthday, a child is set before a table laden with a great number of delicacies and also objects from daily life. A spool of thread goes onto the table because, like noodles which are already there, it symbolizes long life. Uncooked rice and money are put on the table in a wish for wealth, jujubes for many children, a brush and ink stick for good writing, books for outstanding scholarship. (I think we placed a pencil, too.) A ruler is placed on a baby girl's table so that she can grow up to be a good seamstress. On a boy's table, there is also a bow and arrow in a wish for valor. Everyone holds their breath waiting to see what the child picks up first, because that is indicative of the future. If the child grabs money or rice first, then it is going to be very rich, and if it grabs a book, it is going to be a good scholar.

Rice cake includes *paeksŏlgi* (white rice cake), and sometimes rainbow cake and *songp'yŏn* (half-moon shaped, pine-flavored rice cake). The one cake that should never be left out is sorghum balls (*susu kyŏng-dan*), which is said to be the favorite of Grandma Samshin, the goddess that takes care of children. If sorghum balls are made every year until the child becomes nine years old, Grandma Samshin will protect it so well that it would not be injured even if it falls down. Superstition or not, why not make it every year when it is so simple to make anyway?

Fruits are piled up by kind on separate plates.

Hye-jun's First Birthday table was quite impressive thanks to the array of fruit. American grocery stores have all kinds of fruit throughout the year! I think it was also a great idea to cleverly layer the cookies children love. The colorful cookies made a pretty addition to the table and greatly improved the photographs. Nevertheless, I am against layering food into huge pyramids on the First Birthday table as if it were a Sixtieth Birthday table.

All I did for Hye-jun's birthday was prepare food. You and your husband did the rest of it so well, layering the food, setting up the balloons with birthday wishes and fanciful decorations that I could never have imagined when I was your age. It almost broke my heart to tear those pretty decorations off the wall after the party.

Remember the sorghum balls we bought at the store turned out to be glutinous rice balls rolled in sweet bean powder? They explained they did it on purpose because sorghum balls would harden and become inedible very quickly. I was so upset at their unsolicited kindness because the point was not in eating them but in having them there. Because the First Birthday of your second child is coming around and also because you are going to help your sister when she has her baby, I would like to show you an easy way to make sorghum balls. They do not harden so easily and taste quite good.

Sorghum Balls *Susu kyŏngdan,* 수수경단

glutinous sorghum powder
boiling water
salt
sweet bean powder

Mix 1 tablespoon salt in 5 cups glutinous sorghum powder and 1 cup glutinous rice powder and add $1\frac{1}{2}$ cups boiling water. You need much less water if you use fresh powder from the mill (*ttŏk pang-agan*) because it is still moist. (The miller might have added salt, so taste it before mixing the salt in.) Knead well until it becomes like dumpling dough. Shape it into flat palm-size circles and make a hole in the center.

Bring salted water to a boil and add the circles. They are cooked when they float to the top. Take the circles out with a slotted spoon and place them in a mortar or, if you don't have one, in a metal bowl. Beat the circles into a mass with a pestle. Wait until it cools a little. Wet your hands with water, make the cooked dough into bite-size balls, and roll them in the sweet bean powder. The reason you should wait until the dough cools is because the balls become shapeless if you roll them when it is still hot, and of course, you don't want to burn your hands. The balls made this way won't harden that fast. I learned it by chance from some cooking column, and it really worked as it said.

You can make the red bean powder by roasting the red bean paste (*p'atso*) on page 154. Or boil sweet beans until tender to touch, drain, put the beans back in the pan, add salt, and mash with a spatula.

Preparing a baby's First Birthday is the privilege of the mother. I was very happy when you asked me to help you. It was good to split the work so each could do what she did best. We made quite a deal of food between us, which was good because we had so many of our friends over. These days some people do the First Birthday at hotels and big restaurants. I wonder if they know what a First Birthday really is.

The menu on that day consisted of mustard salad (*kyŏjach'ae*) as an appetizer; mixed vegetables (*chapch'ae*) for warm vegetables; acorn jelly (*tot'ori muk*) for cold vegetables; braised pork ribs (*toeji kalbi kangjŏng*) for *tchim*; broiled beef (*soegogi sanjŏk*) for *kui*; mung bean pancakes (*pindaettŏk*) and shrimp in beaten egg (*saeu chŏn*) for *chŏnya*; cold slices of chicken (*tak p'yŏnyuk*) for *p'yŏnyuk*; seaweed soup (*miyŏk kuk*); various kinds of rice cake (*ttŏk*); fermented rice drink (*shik'ye*); sweet rice (*yakshik*); and an assortment of fruit.

It is a good idea to write down what you made so that you can do the same for your next child. Hye-jun picked up a pencil first and then money, didn't she?

Sorghum Balls
Susu Kyŏngdan

dish (*kujŏlp'an*)

Chŏnya: Mung bean pancakes (*pindaettŏk*)

P'yŏnyuk: Beef jelly (*chokp'yŏn*)

Fresh vegetables: Acorn jelly (*tot'ori muk*), bellflower root (*toraji saengch'ae*)

Cooked vegetables: Sautéed cucumber (*oi paetturi*), mixed vegetables (*chapch'ae*)

Tchim: Braised ribs (*kalbi tchim*), braised sea cucumber (*haesamt'ang*)

Kui: Broiled beef (*soegogi kui, pulgogi*)

Soup: White radish soup (*mu kuk*), fancy pot (*shinsŏllo*)

Desserts: Sweet rice (*yakshik*), fermented rice drink (*shik'ye*), rice cake (*ttŏk*), fruit

Children's Birthdays

Mung bean pan cakes (*pindaettŏk*)

Meat patties (*wanja chŏn*)

Fried chicken wings

Barbecued beef kabob

Laver rolls (*kim pap*)

Seaweed soup (*miyŏk kuk*)

Birthday cake and, up to 9th birthday, sorghum balls (*susu kyŏngdan*)

Grown-up's Birthdays

Appetizer: Mustard salad (*kyŏjach'ae*), nine-section

You don't need to do all of the aforementioned, but just a few. I choose sophisticated dishes when I invite in-laws and simpler things when I invite young people.

Koreans must have seaweed soup (*miyŏk kuk*) on their birthdays because, I guess, it is the first soup they had in this world, though indirectly through their mothers who had it and no other soup, meal after meal, for three weeks after child birth to help her recover and produce enough milk. However, it is replaced by white radish soup (*mu kuk*) when one is past sixty.

189

Braised Sea Cucumber
Haesamt'ang, 해삼탕

2 cups soaked sea cucumber
½ pound (1 cup) ground pork
2 bamboo shoots
5 oak mushrooms (**p'yogo**)
5 leaves Korean cabbage
ginger, garlic, green onions, Hoisin sauce, oyster sauce, sugar, corn starch, wine, beef or chicken broth

1. Cut soaked sea cucumber to bite size pieces to make 2 cups. (I can't say how many sea cucumbers because they vary in size when soaked. Two sea cucumbers, identical in size when dry, can be very different when soaked, sometimes one becomes five times as big as the other.)

2. To 5 cups water, add 2 stalks green onion, 2 or 3 slices ginger and 1 tablespoon wine. Bring to a boil and add sea cucumbers. Boil for 5 minutes and drain.

3. To 1 cup ground pork, add 1 teaspoon salt, 2 tablespoons beaten egg, and 1 teaspoon ginger juice. Mix well. Add 1 tablespoon corn starch, mix again. Make balls (the meat will be enough for 8 to 10 balls) and fry. The meat balls need not be perfect. The easy way is to hold the pork mixture in one hand and squeeze it out between the thumb and index fingers. Spoon it off with the other hand and drop into the boiling oil.

4. Pour a little oil in a pre-heated Chinese wok and stir-fry sliced bamboo shoots, sliced oak mushroom and cabbage leaves cut into 1-inch pieces. When the vegetables are cooked, remove them.

5. Pour 2 tablespoons of oil in the wok and fry 2 teaspoons chopped garlic, then add 1 tablespoon Hoisin sauce and mix well. Add 1 tablespoon wine and when the mixture boils, add 1 tablespoon oyster sauce and 1 teaspoon sugar and stir. Then add 1 cup broth and bring to a boil, add the sea cucumber, pork balls and vegetables. Bring to a quick boil, add corn starch liquid (mixture of 1 tablespoon corn starch and 1 tablespoon water), and bring to a boil again. Turn off the heat and add 1 teaspoon sesame oil before serving.

Note

The reason the soaked sea cucumbers are boiled with green onions, ginger and wine in the first place is to remove their odor. The vegetables need not go into this recipe but they are good to increase the volume. Sea cucumbers alone cost too much. Bell peppers, mussels and squid are also good additions.

People who think sea cucumbers are repulsive take them well when meat is added like this. When you don't have Chinese bean paste, soy sauce will do (2 tablespoons).

How to soak dried sea cucumbers

When you buy dried sea cucumbers, choose black ones with pointed warts. Smooth skinned ones are tasteless. In a clean pan without any trace of oil, pour warm water and soak sea cucumbers. Bring to a boil and turn off the heat. Wait until the water cools and see if the sea cucumbers have become soft enough for cutting. Slit the sea cucumbers lengthwise and clean them of innards and mud. Soak the cleaned sea cucumbers in fresh water and boil. Let cool and boil again in the same water. Repeat until they soften, removing those which softened first and keeping them in cold water.

Seasonal Festivals and Family Get-Togethers

New Year's Day *Sŏlnal,* 설날

Rice-cake soup (*ttŏk kuk*)
Dumpling soup (*mandu kuk*)
A variety of pan-fried food (*chŏnya*)
Braised meat (*tchim*)
Broiled or roasted meat (*kui*)
Vegetables (*namul*)
Fermented rice drink (*shik'ye*) or
Persimmon punch (*sujŏnggwa*),
Rice cake
Fruit

You can add dumplings to the rice-cake soup to make rice-cake/dumpling soup (*ttŏk mandu kuk*).

For people who do not like the two mixed together, I steam dumplings separately.

The Eighth Full Moon *Ch'usŏk,* 추석

Freshly harvested rice
Taro soup
Tchim
Sanjŏk
An assortment of *chŏnya*
Three different colored vegetables (*namul*)
White radish and cabbage *kimch'i* (*nabak kimch'i*)
Korean cabbage *kimch'i* (*paech'u kimch'i*)

Pine-flavored rice cakes (*songp'yŏn*)
Fruit

I make radish soup flavored with tashima instead of taro soup because we don't like it much. I get itchy all over when I have taro soup.

When I was growing up, *Chusŏk* was not properly celebrated if *songp'yŏn* were not made. It is still so in many Korean homes. Men become quite cooperative around *songp'yŏn* making time. Children also like to make them. It is quite heartwarming with all the family working and having a fun time together, as long as you have not made so much of the dough that you wear out everyone's enthusiasm.

On Thanksgiving Day, which is an American version of our *Chusŏk*, I prepared a turkey, vegetables *(namul)*, an assortment of *chŏnya* and soup, when I was in the States. I also made a pumpkin pie because it seemed to be a Thanksgiving must in America and also because it was universally liked, even by those not so keen about pumpkins.

Rice-cake Soup
Ttŏk kuk

193

The most important get-together of our family, next to birthdays and memorial days, takes place on Children's Day (May 5 in Korea). Since we moved to Kihŭng, all the children in the family and their parents come to our house. When it rains on Children's Day, we meet on the following Sunday. Both children and parents enjoy themselves thoroughly. I hope Hye-jun will soon join the children. I am sure she would love it.

Because everyone brings their children there are easily more than 30 people. I get busy about two weeks beforehand. Prizes should be bought and wrapped, the garden should be festooned with balloons and little flags, games and play sets should be hauled out of storage, and of course there are foods to be prepared. Confined in the hustle bustle of Seoul the year round, our city-dwelling relatives really appreciate a day of feasting and frolicking outdoors. Your father believes the day is as important to the parents as to their children because it brings everyone closer and reminds them of the importance of family.

My belief, however, is that no matter how great the programs he prepares are, they won't get half as good results if the food isn't good. I prepare a buffet in the garden with *pindaettŏk, wanja chŏn, chapch'ae, tot'ori muk, kalbi tchim* (braised ribs), *tak p'yŏnyuk* (chicken slices), fried dumplings, *kim pap* (laver rolls), and kabobs to barbecue. For dinner, I always make *naengmyŏn* (cold noodles).

Treating some 30 or 40 people to two meals in a row, I have to prepare food for almost a hundred. By the time everyone leaves, I am exhausted but have a great feeling of satisfaction.

Christmas

After many years of rather desolate Christmas by ourselves, it was exciting to have Hi-chang and his wife Su-jin with us last Christmas. For the Christmas dinner, I overwhelmed them by making all of the traditional Korean foods they liked: nine-section dish (*kujŏlp'an*), stuffed cucumber (*oisŏn*), mixed vegetables (*chapch'ae*), various kinds of *chŏnya*, beef jelly (*chokp'yŏn*), broiled beef, fancy pot (*shinsŏllo*), fermented rice drink (*shik'ye*), and honey cookies (*yakkwa*). The last I had made in advance.

Though it involves a great deal of work, making the nine-section dish has some advantage because if you prepare more ingredients than you need, you will have already prepared enough for *chapch'ae* and *shinsŏllo* as well. Part of the *chŏnya* can also go into the *shinsŏllo*. The beef jelly (*chokp'yŏn*) takes time and effort, however.

When children bother you while you are cooking, get them busy helping. Children play better fiddling with food preparations than with toys and remain quiet until they are finished with what they were given to do. I learned that trick at your husband's cub scout meeting where parents helped make Christmas decorations.

If your friends drop by without warning, wouldn't it be nice to treat them to a meal? For lunch, you could simply make noodles mixed with *kimch'i* (*pibim kuksu*) and some broth and for dinner, add one or two extra side dishes—nothing in the gourmet line—to whatever you had planned for your meal. I think the best and the most memorable way to make friends is to eat together and especially at home.

What with the hectic pace of life and the difficulty in getting help, it is not as easy as in the good old days to have a get-together at home. It would be much easier if everyone could contribute a dish. Indeed, it seems American pot luck is gaining popularity among young people in Korea these days. I am sure you have been to such an event a number of times, but just for your reference in case you host one at your house, set up the table and prepare rice, soup, *kimch'i* and drinks together with enough ice and let the visitors bring one dish per person. The hostess should work out a list of foods in advance and organize everything so that everyone won't bring the same thing.

For a picnic, how about rice cooked at home, *pulgogi*, lettuce, fresh green peppers, and bean and red pepper paste sauce for dipping (*ssamjang*)? Wash the vegetables at home and bring them in plastic bags. As for *pulgogi*, season the beef at home so it is ready to barbecue at the picnic site. If you want sandwiches, pack the spreads in a plastic container and make sandwiches on the site. For stew (*tchigae*), simmer meat, vegetables, seasoning, bean paste and red pepper paste all together at home. All you have to do at the picnic is pour water on the mixture and boil.

Gifts of Food

Koreans have a tradition of sending money or other gifts called *pujo* to weddings, funerals, 60th birthdays and other important occasions. When I got married, friends and relatives congratulated me with things they thoughtfully chose to help set up a new home, but these days everyone makes *pujo* in money. Nevertheless, I try to make *pujo* in food whenever I can because it is more helpful.

My friend Ko Song-suk contributed noodles at your wedding. They were so useful that I keep thanking her even now. She not only boiled the noodles, made the soup they were to go in and beef and vegetable garnishes to put on them, but also came over and served them herself. The noodles were very delicious. And think of all the time and effort and, above all, her good heart to volunteer for such a major task. She saved me a great deal of work.

Sending flowers to a family in mourning is not a bad idea but they really appreciate a gift of porridge for the bereaved and food for people at the wake. Food to take to the grave site is even more appreciated. It will make a very good contribution if each of the family friends pitches in with one kind of food.

I will list useful foods just in case you have occasions to make a food contribution.

For weddings, make mung bean pancakes (*pindaettŏk*) garnished with green leaves of garland chrysanthemum and red pepper slices, noodles, and/or an assortment of *chŏnya*. You could also make a generous amount of *muk* (acorn jelly). A nine-section dish (*kujŏlp'an*) is not a bad idea, either.

For graveside dining, send dried pollack braised in sauce (*pugŏ chorim*), braised pork (*cheyuk chorim*) or braised pork ribs (*toeji kalbi kangjŏng*), fresh bellflower root salad (*toraji saengch'ae*), pan-fried *pindaettŏk*, pan-fried fish fillets (*saengsŏn chŏn*), meat patties (*wanja chŏn*), *kimch'i*, and/or hot radish *kimch'i* (*kkaktugi*). I cut Korean cabbage *kimch'i* lengthwise, wrap each piece in plastic wrap and cut across to make small chunks so that it would be easy to serve. My friend told me that it was indeed very convenient because she didn't have to cut the *kimch'i* but just served a chunk to each person.

When someone moves to a new house, I send sweet bean porridge (*p'at chuk*) with glutinous rice balls mixed in it.

Living so far away, you have to be away from home a long time if you visit your parents in Korea. This shouldn't be too much of a problem because your husband can cook decent meals, but for your peace of mind I wrote down the kinds of food that you could prepare and keep in the refrigerator for a month.

When we were in the Philippines and also after we moved back to Seoul, I would sometimes travel to the States to be with my sons for a month or so. For your father-in-law who would be left alone, I always made and packed food to last the period I was to be away. We had a maid in the Philippines, but I felt better if I prepared everything myself. I still pack his meals for several days when I go sightseeing with my friends. Because there are just the two of us here, he should be able to cook or at least heat what is already cooked in case I become ill.

Steam dumplings and pack in plastic bags, ten to a bag. Prepare soup, freeze in a plastic container or in individual plastic bags. The meat in the soup should be removed beforehand for seasoning and kept separately beside the soup packs.

Cut the head and tail off salted fish and pack one by one in plastic bags all ready for broiling. Season *pulgogi*, pack just enough for a meal and freeze. Layer sliced beef for roast (*ros kui*) with sheets of plastic wrap between the layers so the meat won't freeze together. To enable your husband to make *chapch'ae*, prepare vegetables and divide them by individual meals. Season and stir-fry beef strips and freeze with the vegetables in a plastic container. Keep the *yangnyŏmjang* separately.

Salt and pepper chicken pieces, deep-fry and keep with *yangnyŏmjang* so that he can make chicken in sauce (*tak tchim*) when he feels like it. Make vegetable soup (Russian soup) and freeze in portions for one meal. Spaghetti sauce frozen in one meal portions is also a good idea because all he will have to do is boil the spaghetti.

I used to make these things and others and stick the menu for everyday on the refrigerator. The plan obviously worked quite nicely because he didn't complain when I called home to check on him from time to time. He even entertained his friends with them. By the time I returned home a month later, there was only a couple of packs left in the freezer.

Ah, well, I think that's about all. I have done my best measuring, tasting and rewriting, but you are always welcome to revise and add. If you find easier ways to make some of the recipes, note them down also. I didn't venture to write anything on Western cooking because you are surely better than me in that area. If you let me know of anything else your husband would like to have, I will send the recipes.

Epilogue

I started working when I finished college. I kept my job after marriage and even after having two children so that we could save enough money for a house of our own. Eventually we bought a house, but by then my husband was sent abroad by his company, and our family began moving first to one country and then to another.

When we lived in the States and later in Indonesia, we had our children with us, but things became complicated when we were sent to the Philippines. Because my husband had to work on a remote island and not in Manila, we decided to send the boys to my sister's in the States for their schooling. My sister was an excellent cook and took good care of my children, but I felt so guilty and useless, only to be able to play mother during their vacation. When the children came home, I cooked everything for them I had practiced during their absence.

For months before their home coming, I would buy cookbook after cookbook and try all the impressive looking recipes, tasting and revising them to suit my taste. When the children finally came, I cooked the foods one after another. I wrote down the recipes they liked so that I could make them again the next vacation. For three months I would feed them the best I could. Then the vacation would be over and the children would leave for school again. I couldn't bring myself to eat the foods they liked because even looking at them brought a big lump to my throat.

My children were six and eight years old when we moved to the States the first time. They had trouble with English at first but soon began to use it even at home. I insisted that they speak Korean at home and gave them the hunger treatment and even spanked them if they did not. So that they wouldn't forget Korea and the taste of Korean food, I served Korean food once every day and made special delicacies on Korean seasonal festivals. Because I did not like the quality of rice powder available in Indonesia and the Philippines, I made rice powder myself to make Korean rice cakes for the children. To make rice powder, I soaked rice, ground it in a mortar, sent the liquid through a sieve, squeezed it out in a cotton sack and dried the sediment. I even made mung bean powder to make bean jelly at home.

It is my belief that the best way to remember one's own country is through the language and food. Thanks to my efforts, both my sons married Korean girls. To make my happiness even greater, both of them are daughters of my high school classmates.

My daughters-in-law are both thoughtful girls who call me every week just to say hello. Our conversations invariably end up with talk about food. One time I suggested that they make a list of foods they wanted to make, and I would send them detailed recipes. Letters came and went, each one was filed in the computer. The recipes soon became a small pile when they were printed out. I realized it would make a good wedding gift for the daughters of my friends. After adding a few more recipes, I asked my son to edit and print them for my friends. Then the word spread and things developed so that this cookbook came into being.

I think I owe an apology to my readers for my humble cookbook. It did not start as a real cookbook and still does not have pretty photographs nor recipes for sophisticated dishes. It is not scientifically or nutritionally systematized because I simply wrote down my ways and secrets with the hope of helping my daughters-in-law prepare their daily meals. My only desire was to encourage them to enjoy easy cooking for pleasant meals with their families.

My two daughters-in-law are directly responsible for my writing this book. My eldest son and his wife are thoughtful people, and I am especially thankful for my eldest daughter-in-law, because she always discusses things with everyone in the family before she makes any decisions on family affairs. I am also thankful for my reliable eldest son to whom I know I can turn for help any time, for my younger daughter-in-law who inspires me with her positive thinking, for my second son who lectured me on my poor computer work and then reorganized my collection of recipes himself, from the table of contents to page numbering, and finally for my husband who always encourages me to do whatever I want to do.

Chang Sun-young
From Kihŭng
November 15, 1993

"Where's Grandpa?" Hye-jun asks.

"He's gone to Seoul. You know what he took to go to Seoul?"

"Airp'ane."

"Where's Grandma, Hye-jun?"

"In Seoul. Grandma's making noodles."

Even to her little granddaughter, the most vivid image of my mother-in-law seems to be that of her cooking. The first thing she does when she flies over to see her darling granddaughter is to make *kimch'i*. No sooner than she's unpacked her luggage, she's off to a Korean supermarket to buy a box of Korean cabbage and radish.

Like any other American kitchen, the kitchen in my house was never designed with *kimch'i* making in mind. To make things worse, the sink is far too high for my petite mother-in-law. Nevertheless, she makes heaps of *kimch'i*, enough to last the whole winter for an ordinary family, and she does that single-handedly regardless of season, cleaning, washing, salting and stuffing all by herself. At first, my job at such times was that of an apprentice, cleaning green onions and peeling garlic, but that was when I did not have children. The biggest help I offer nowadays is to keep my two children away from the kitchen while she works.

Mother's *kimch'i*, which she seasons and stuffs "primitively" without the use of plastic gloves to protect her hands from the spices because of her belief in the importance of the hands-on touch, is always fresh and tasty as if it came out of a new jar of winter *kimch'i*. Besides, her *kimch'i* is always the same, not once too salty or too bland. The secret of her consistency she says is the "scientific" way of measuring every ingredient accurately.

The delicious, scientifically made *kimch'i* is packed in every *kimch'i* container in the house to become our major staple for two months and also priceless gifts for our friends in the neighborhood. By now I have a long list of friends who are eagerly looking forward to her *kimch'i* gift. Mother loves to share food, but not just making gifts of food, she loves to invite people over and treat them with homemade food. It is quite natural that everybody who knows her always thinks of delicious food at the mention of her name.

This does not mean that Mother can do nothing but cook. She is an excellent calligrapher who has taught classes and has a great knowledge of music and literature. She was a member of a university drama group and worked for the university newspaper. During her extensive stay abroad, she even learned ballet with children. Petite as she is, Mother is also an accomplished golfer and swimmer. With all of her versatility, why is it that she is always remembered for her cooking? I think it is because of her generosity that makes her always willing to give.

Mother seldom uses chemical additives. The one additive she likes to use and uses in abundance is her caring heart. I had much to learn when I thought cooking was a matter of the right ingredients processed according to the right procedure. Now I know no food tastes right unless it is prepared with the additive called "care."

To quote a popular Korean adage, "a school dog can recite a poem after three years of being a school dog." Having lived under Mother's wing for more than four years, I daresay I am doing better than a school dog in the field of cooking. Yet I am very uncomfortable cooking in front of Mother. It is even harder than speaking in English in front of my brother-in-law's wife. (She was an English teacher in Korea.) I get so nervous that I can't get simple things that I usually cook without a hitch to taste right. She makes me even more nervous by eating all of my miserable cooking with relish.

I think she has written this cookbook for me instead of chiding me for my failures. It is her gentle way of teaching the family tradition and cooking to her sons and daughters-in-law who live apart from her.

I must confess that Mother's particularities in cooking caused me quite a bit of stress. I thought she was obsessed with food and complained that her attitude was breaking the balance among food, clothing and shelter for our family. I vowed that I would not be like her, but unbeknownst to myself, I must have been brainwashed because I find myself thinking of cooking ever more often. My suspicion is confirmed by my friends who comment on my cooking saying, "like mother-in-law, like daughter-in-law."

Mother always teaches us in a roundabout way like that. She would send us without comment books like *Manners and Tradition of a Family*, a collection of essays on an exemplary family life. Instead of finding fault, she induces us to realize what we did wrong ourselves by praising what we did well. In fact, she constantly speaks so highly of her daughters-in-law that I keep blushing with embarrassment, but I know she does so out of the hope that we will become worthy of all her praises.

Last summer when I visited her in Seoul with my children, Mother one day asked, "What do you want for lunch? *Naengmyŏn*, dumplings or noodles?" I answered noodles thinking that was the simplest of the three to make. I thought she would open a pack of dry noodles and boil them, but was I mistaken. She took out flour and began to make a dough.

That was typical of Mother's cooking. She starts from kneading the dough when she makes noodles, from drying fresh red peppers for pepper powder when making *kimch'i*. Done with care every step of the way, Mother's cooking is truly a work of art.

I ask my eldest daughter who is playing house with her little sister of less than 10 months, "What are you doing, Hye-jun?"

"I'm making *pindaettŏk*. You wanna some, Mama?"

Yi Chong-mun
Chang Sun-young's Eldest Daughter-in-Law

Index

음식 이름 찾아보기